The Last Inquisitor

A Novel

by Mikaela Mar and Daniel Aharoni

ISBN: 1-5882-0467-7

This book is printed on acid free paper.

1stBooks - rev. 02/14/02

ONE

The Inquisitor looked in the mirror propped above the chipped bathroom sink. Today, he found his face intolerably sad.

He started to shave.

He used an old fashioned razor, an army razor that doubled well as a weapon. Between each stroke, he dipped the long blade in water and waited until it shed its human debris. His hands moved deliberately, prompted by an inner rhythm that controlled his rage.

The newspaper article left no doubt. Catherine Kemeny's nomination for Deputy Attorney General for Human Rights was imminent.

Why did he let her live? If someone pointed to him now, it was over. To think they had assured him he was safe. "Just watch your back with The Fifth. From us you've got nothing to fear, all records are destroyed," they said.

How about now? How about Kemeny?

His hand pressed hard against the blade. The mirror reflected the single 40 watt bulb, just enough light to see the cracked turquoise tile. Everything around him was gaping, wounded, torn apart. Except for the mirror, and his face. Through some miracle, they had both remained intact.

"Lesson number one, Vorody. Torture is necessary." He can still hear the words of comrade Lidoevsky — Liddy. They are both about the same age, mid-twenties. This is Grigor's first assignment at Lubyanka. Liddy has been around Stalin's political prison much longer. He graduated almost four years before from KGB academy. "They got me straight from the crib," he jokes, rolling a Black Russian. When he smokes, his eyes narrow with pleasure and his moon-shaped cheeks smile. He always smiles. Liddy is the funny man around KGB headquarters. The problem with him is he expects torture victims to laugh at his jokes too.

Lubyanka is big and yellow, situated like a giant oozing sore right in the middle of Moscow. People look like crawling bugs when they walk in front of the Soviet fortress, going about their business, trying to forget that behind those walls men and women die without knowing if outside it is night or day.

Liddy takes Grigor's first victim from the "stone bag". That's a cell Pavlov, the big boss, designed himself. Very tall, narrow, no windows. Nothing in it, just a little bench. You can't stretch your arms to the side, Grigor knows, because they locked him up in one of those once, in training. There is no air at first. But you live. You always live. Because there is no light and all is black around you, and because you want to live, you imagine you are on a boat at night in the middle of the ocean. The boat swings gently in the wind, rides the crests of the waves. The idea of movement makes it possible to breathe again.

The victim is a young man. He keeps his eyes wide open when he's out in the snow and sun, like an idiot. So now he can't see for a while and his eyes hurt.

He uses the ice box on this one, which is not so great because you have to freeze your ass too, except you're dressed in fur and the prisoner is naked on the ice, sprayed with cold water. You watch a man turn into a popsicle in about twenty minutes. If you don't get what you want out of him fast he's got to go back or he goes into shock. A lot of them do. Then they go to the prison hospital and then back to the stone bag and to another torture until they talk. Afterwards, if they're lucky, they go to a hard labor camp. Liddy laughs at Grigor because he stops the torture too soon. He tells him a joke about frozen testicles and just before he can say the punch line the prisoner dies.

"God it was awful," the Inquisitor murmured, wiping his pale cheeks and the foggy mirror with a clean, white towel. Everything was awful. The cold in Moscow, the food, Liddy, his desk, Father's letters, straight out of a Marxist textbook, the soldier who spilled bean soup on his brown leather holster, and the smell of death which even now, after all these years, still clung to him like filth.

He wiped the last drop of foam gathered in the crease of his upper lip. The taste of soap filled his mouth. He spit twice in the sink and cursed, in Russian. Perhaps he will decide to grow a mustache today.

Or kill Catherine Kemeny.

A photograph of him before he came to America still hung above the mirror — at first he couldn't destroy it in case he'd need it later. And now he just kept it there, a thumbtack piercing the forehead of a man even he could not recognize. This was the only picture he ever let them take of him — a passport photograph. He wore his hair very straight and groomed then, like a Chinaman. And black rimmed glasses he had them make especially for him, with thick, clear glass. It had been a worthwhile disguise, except it lasted longer, much longer than he expected. He was unrecognizable five years ago at the border crossing in Miami, with his naked face framed by natural, overgrown curls.

"Passport — American. Name — Gregory Varda."

But two years later he was recognized. The face that served him well for 30 years betrayed him twice.

The thought even now, especially now, swelled in his chest, painfully.

"Lesson number two, Vorody. Mistakes are fatal."

"Fatal for whom?" he replied out loud, to the memory.

"The Inquisitor is still here, alive and well. Look at me."

But the mirror disappeared in the steam rising from the electric samovar. He shrugged and inhaled the bitter aroma of black tea. Nowadays he had to do this in the bathroom, the only room that still had running water and electricity.

"Everyone around you dies and you don't. Because You are Necessary."

One of the pigeons he chose back then was a woman with breast cancer. Her family in Israel was paying to send her to the United States for treatment, but she needed an exit visa. She was desperate.

When he met her, he played a Russian named Rostov, working in Hungary with the military, who offered to help her arrange a passport. He planted the military information he wanted her to deliver as soon as she reached the United States. Pigeons always traded inside knowledge for political asylum. His Human Ministry banked on human predictability.

She was quite ill when he visited her that second time in her low hospital bed at Cancer Ward. He had arranged to have her alone in a large room normally reserved for six, not that the beds were not needed. On the contrary, but his mission required privacy. He took a good look at her in the dim light. He was probably wasting his time. She looked like she might not make it after all.

He was reluctant to sit beside her at first, the proximity of a death he had not inflicted startled him. But there were no chairs. He sat on a narrow patch of her bed and she smiled. Somehow from then on things seemed easy.

He spoke with her for a long time about her life and his fictitious adventures in the military. He remembered being carried away by her youth and her vague, drifting beauty. After he told her she could leave the country as soon as she was able, she held his hand and thanked him, endlessly. He felt faint, because her hair smelled of the sweet perfume Mother used when they lived at the embassy. She insisted that they hug. He let her hold him for a moment, unwillingly. His glasses got caught in the lace of her robe and when he bent down to pick them up, her kiss fell on the corner of his lips. He waited to leave the room, trying not to swallow or open his mouth before he could spit and wipe it with his handkerchief.

Normally, pigeons were disposed of immediately after delivery. But this one never delivered. She never went to immigration with the military secrets. She went to Bethesda, Maryland, instead. She got her treatment, lived and healed, while he kept waiting for her to talk. After a while, he gave up on the woman. But he decided not to terminate. An exception. The unsuccessful pigeon had earned her life.

3

Ten years later he was coming out of the Ziegfield, a movie theater in Manhattan. He liked to see movies when no one was around, at the first matinee.

And there she was, looking healthy, fit. She recognized him at once.

"My God, Mr. Rostov," she cried, huge tears streaming down her face, as if they had been waiting, bottled all that time.

He turned his back and walked away quickly, hoping she would think she made a mistake.

"Mr. Rostov" she came running after him, grabbing his hand, making him turn to face her, "My darling Mister Rostov, look at me, remember me? I was dying and you saved me!"

He could not believe the transformation. The last time he saw her she had death perched on her shoulder, waiting to take her away. Now she was forty, and alive. Beautiful, and alive.

"You know Mr. Rostov, I can tell you now that the communists are gone. When I applied for my refugee status I never said a bad word about Hungary — or about any of the military things you've told me," she whispered in his ear proudly. "Your secret is still with me."

So that was the mystery. The pigeon protected the executioner. She had saved her own life. Grigor grew suddenly weary of lying. What the hell of a difference did it make if this woman knew he was in New York? Who the hell cared any more? And who was she going to tell so late in the game?

She would have done anything to thank him for getting her the passport, for getting her to New York and the treatment that gave her back her life. He took her to his hotel suite and peeled her clothes off piece by piece, wanting to feel her warmth, her life, that precious life that seemed so earned, so important, afraid to look at the scar where her breast had been, afraid to be reminded how she lay dying in the empty cancer ward, without anyone to share her pain, and how he plotted to take advantage of her misery. But he had to look. And then he couldn't stop looking. Because it was beautiful. Her scar was a scar of hope. And the one breast she had left, perfect, ripe, whole, was her triumph. Good triumphed over evil in the end. She made him feel an unexpected happiness that lingered with him long after they said good bye.

She wanted to see him again. He gave her a fake telephone number and left for Chicago the same day. She should have been terminated right then and there. But this time he could not.

Then the woman talked. She went and told her friends about her life savior and their passionate night. She fell in love with her hero. She looked for him everywhere, asking questions of everyone. The hotel. The police. The Hungarian Embassy.

4

If cancer didn't kill her, gratitude did. An overdose of sedatives — perhaps there was news the cancer had returned? No one could know. She was lucky to have lived those ten years, her friends whispered at the final ceremony.

The second time he was recognized was less personal, but much more dangerous. This time it was one of his lieutenants in the Human Ministry.

Vorody assigned the termination of a Hungarian dissident writer who lived in Paris to one of his finest men, Ferencz Jonas. He was to use an umbrella tipped in untraceable poison during the writer's daily Metro ride to his French publisher.

Vorody knew Jonas's former girlfriend had defected to Italy after traveling there with the Budapest circus. She was a trapeze star. Jonas could never hope to get out of the country after that because his motivations to defect were considered strong. But the woman had left two years before, and Jonas had a spotless record. He was an ace at setting up informer networks, ruthless and cruel, Vorody's favorite enforcer in interrogations and torture. Besides, he was attractive and a string of women pigeons reported he was heartless and played the field. None believed Jonas had any loyalties to the former girlfriend.

He disobeyed his own rules.

Jonas never went for the kill. He went straight to the French government, spilled his guts about the assignment and was passed on to the Americans for debriefing and relocation. The trapeze artist had been the culprit after all. CIA made sure he told everything he knew. Pavlov was mad.

Ferencz Jonas showed up years later at the Fontainbleau Hilton in Miami at a surveillance convention for private detectives and security companies. He still wondered why he went there himself. Withdrawal, he presumed.

The Inquisitor knew Ferencz Jonas recognized him long before he slid out from of his aisle seat. He followed him, unseen, unheard, a panther back on the trail, hating what had to be done, blaming his former soldier for his stupidity.

Outside, under the blood-red sky, Vorody watched Ferencz Jonas, who loved a trapeze artist more than he loved his own life, rush to his rented car and speed away. He trailed him on his motorcycle to Little Havana through frantic dead turns and twists, letting his prey hope that he could lose himself in the neon city. He stood outside an ornate Cuban restaurant watching the man he once trusted eat his last meal. Through the windows came the faint sound of merengue and the courtly dance of overweight maidens in golden dresses who served men in white shirts from large jugs of pink wine. Jonas drank fast and ate slowly, glancing now and then at the glistening darkness outside. Little Havana was as far as he could go before fate caught up to him.

Maybe Jonas didn't know the Inquisitor was near, but when he stepped out on the hot asphalt that burned his feet as if they were bare, he shuddered. That night the street was rowdy with drunken sailors and half-naked whores. The birds were asleep, and the palm trees took the wind in stride making a rough, broken sound. The sea was high. Predators came out to hunt.

The Inquisitor waited in the shadow. He looked his victim in the eye as he approached and, wordless, crushed his neck with one sharp, controlled move. Not even a gasp disturbed the passing of the man who thought he could betray Grigor Vorody.

He placed his dead soldier in the passenger seat. "Boracho, hombre, dead drunk" a homeless Cuban laughed and walked past the rented car without looking back. He started to drive south, on the interstate highway.

They say alligators eat anything that you put in their way, if you break into their territory. They say you'll know when you reach that place because the road leads nowhere. It stops abruptly, without warning, and before you there is nothing but a vast, infinite stretch of swamp. You know then that you've reached the end of Miami, the end of America, maybe even the end of the world as you know it. The furthermost tip of the Everglades.

It's at that exact spot alligator kingdom starts.

Even children know not to cross the invisible line to where the alligators nest. Still, on nights with a full moon, the odd tourist, hypnotized by the magic of the swamp or simply dead drunk, might step by mistake onto their path.

The ten foot beasts come out at night from the muddy waters and lie, alert and dangerous, on the road, right where a car might stop. Savage, primordial, each day they gain another inch of the territory that still belongs to man. So the swamp grows bigger, stronger, noisier, teeming with a life that is infinite and indestructible. There, at the end of the continent, the beasts prevail.

Vorody undressed the lifeless body of Ferencz Jonas and placed it carefully, respectfully, right there, at the edge of the alligator trail. The naked head and shoulders touched the water and the white flesh glistened indecently in the moonlight. He burned the clothes on a patch of quicksand and waited until he could bury the ashes. When he drove again by the end trail the white intruder was gone. Somewhere a primeval beast had helped ease Ferencz Jonas into eternity.

The car, reeking of alcohol, was found the next day perched precariously off the road into the swamp, which made the inquiry into the disappearance and death of the improbable visitor conclude it was an accident. Tourists took forbidden routes, and if they drove inebriated at God knows what speed at a late hour, the swamp was known to draw them with its slippery ways. No one ever found bodies in the swamp. No one even had the nerve to try.

And now there she was, the Inquisitor thought, swallowing the memory with another sip of black Russian tea.

The third intruder.

Catherine Kemeny.

TWO

President Stone was having a lousy day, and it was still only half over. First thing in the morning, the lumber industry calls him the Prince of Deceit. Screaming at the press conference about campaign promises. Accusing him of job cuts in the interest of tree worshipers. He had to thank the venerable Cyrus Moses from Washington state for inciting that one.

He picked up the phone and punched the first code.

"Larry. Listen. How come we're dealing with the lumber industry right now? Why'd you go ahead and announce it before I gave the O.K.?"

"But you approved it, Bob."

"When?"

"In March. I told you I wanted to make it one of my issues and you said go."

"But why now? I thought we'd decided we didn't need another national controversy at the moment. My plate's pretty full. Larry?"

Silence. The President sighed.

"It's all right, it's all right. Don't worry about it. Just brief me on all the implications from now on. I have to study this carefully now that they're on our backs. And Larry — better be well researched this time. I don't want to look like an idiot."

Why did he let Devane off the hook again? He couldn't help wondering. Well, the vice president did bring in the cash and the Southern vote.

Next, he buzzed Marvin Krone, his Chief of Staff. No luck. He had already gone to the lobby to greet the human rights nominee. God, he was running late, again. He skimmed quickly through the Russia file. They wanted the money he had promised Yeltsin. The phone rang on Direct One. It was Millicent.

"Honey, what's up?" he said, trying to squelch his irritation. Her voice came at him in waves, like nausea, from the cellular phone in her car.

"What?" He could barely hear her.

"The National Rehabilitation Program? No, Millie, I told you, they're doing a feasibility study."

"What? I know I promised, but I can't just —"

"Hello?"

"Georgie's running a fever? Did you call the doctor?"

"Millie? Millie? What? I can't hear you."

Dammit, she must have gone through a tunnel. Either that or she hung up.

He turned back to the Russia file. What did that reporter ask him that morning? "Mr. President. Don't the problems we have at home warrant your

8

attention and our money more than the Russians'?" They did. They certainly did. But how the hell could he solve all the world's problems in one day? Yeltsin had called before breakfast, as always, telling him he was counting on his word. He told him not to worry, but now he had to reconsider. What about politics? What about pressures from within? And what about the worth of a man's word in the scheme of things?

He dialed the next call on Direct One. He hated to do this, but how could he avoid it? Saddam had acted up again last night and his defense chief just resigned. If only Larry Devane was as capable as he was rich, the President would have had a shoulder to lean on. Even an elbow would be nice.

The former President of the United States answered the phone, sounding enviably mellow.

"Bob, what a pleasure. Are you taking good care of my house?"

"Jack. Pleasure's all mine. The White House looks great. Rose garden especially."

"I was expecting your call."

"You were?"

"Well. I heard about Saddam."

Just then Direct Two started beeping.

"Yes. Well. Jack. I can't really fathom this one. We've done absolutely nothing to upset him. We've given him the message that we want peace and quiet around here, Jack."

"How many this time?'

"Five. The pilot, and the boys on surveillance. And of course we lost the plane."

Direct Two beeped now periodically, like an alarm clock. It gathered steam every time. That's how they built the damned things around here. Just in case he tried to ignore them.

"Listen, Jack, can I call you in five?"

"I think we better meet Bob — you need a plan, and fast."

The beeper was driving him out of his mind.

"Yes. Tomorrow. Tenish? Devane will be with me. And the national security staff. I'll send the plane for you at 7 am sharp."

"Yes well, I'd like Converse there too, from CIA Operations."

"Sure thing Jack. I appreciate this. Thanks, Jack."

Direct Two went off just as he picked up. Damn. It must be urgent. No one called him on that line unless there was a fire somewhere. They'd call back.

Direct One lit up. He picked up.

His wife's voice suddenly chilled him.

"Bob, did you hang up on me?"

"Yes, Mill, I thought you …"

"Bob, don't hang up on me. The rehab fund is my biggest commitment. You know that."

"Millie, listen to me, please. You know that I respect your mission. Getting those crack mothers and their babies in rehab communities is —"

"It's my life, Stone."

"Well, it's my life, too, Millie. But it's gonna cost a bundle."

"Get rid of an army base if you have to."

"It's not that easy, Mill, and you know it. They're doing a feasibility study to see how much money we'll need for the medical arm. And then there's the vocational rehab. Hell, the housing alone —"

Her voice was like a cold shower.

"I'm not letting you off the hook."

"Millie, try to understand —"

She hung up.

Krone stepped in, bald, sturdy and efficient. Stone sighed.

"The wife, Sir? Acting up?"

Stone looked at him, displeased.

"Tell me about the human rights nominee."

"Do you want to see the video?"

Stone nodded, and pulled the heavy curtains while Krone started the tape.

He settled in his chair enjoying the moment of darkness. He liked the oval office like this, barely lit by the flicker of the screen. It had magic. His chair, the desk, the tall mahogany book case glistening in the dark, the thick Aubusson rug spotted here and there by a bright dot where daylight managed to peek through antique burgundy velvet. Yet even magic could not disguise the reality of this room. Everything was on loan here. It occurred to him that nothing, not even his own life belonged to him anymore.

"The name is Catherine Kemeny — but you know that. Everyone calls her Kay. The press loves her. She doesn't seem to have any skeletons anywhere we looked."

"Did we look everywhere?"

"Could we afford not to?"

A bit cocky, were we not? Stone frowned.

"Go on."

"Background is perfect. Harvard degree, then a career with the U.S. Attorney, then private practice. Made her name defending two major cases you'll see on tape. Then back to the Justice Department as federal prosecutor, working on a series of civil rights cases against high secret police officials from dictatorships, mainly Eastern Europe, on behalf of former victims. Those were closed door cases so there's no footage unless you want to read the transcripts."

Stone shrugged. "Ambitious. Driven. Wants to make a difference. One of the best young lawyers we've got."

The video showed her first in a TV interview. Mid-thirties, elegant, poised. He couldn't see her body at first, but could guess it. Lean and tall. Skin golden, like honey. And an inch-long scar across the left cheek. She flaunted it, he thought. She certainly didn't try to hide it. She was beautiful. Too beautiful. Classy and haughty, reserved. Not his type. But the eyes burned when she spoke, there was fire in there. Great speaker. Even with the sound low he could hear the melodious voice and a faint Hungarian accent.

"Any problems with the accent when you tested?"

"No. None. Immigrants identify with her. Important for the human rights angle. Everyone else goes for the powerful voice and looks. She played well."

"Parents?'

"Father was a famous dissident writer, Nicholas Kemeny. He died in a communist jail in Hungary. She escaped with her mother and uncle and made it here when she was 12. Since then, she's committed herself to human rights."

The President remained quiet, watching one of the cases that made her famous when she was a defense lawyer. It had been recorded documentary style for Court TV. As per the program's format, Kemeny was shown explaining her actions and motivations after the verdict. The case involved a man named Popescu, a naturalized American living in Brooklyn, accused of ordering the revenge killing of another Romanian, a former Securitate Colonel, who was found shot execution style in his apartment on Park Avenue. Twenty years before, the colonel jailed and tortured Popescu, who lost an eye and his freedom at the age of 21. At the time of the Colonel's death, Popescu had a solid alibi, but the police, who had been coincidentally taping the telephone calls of a known Brooklyn mobster who happened to be Popescu's brother-in-law, had recorded an interesting exchange between the two men the day after the murder. The recording was unusually clear, albeit in the Calabrese dialect, which Popescu spoke fairly well after having been married for 18 years into the closely knit Calabrese community of Brooklyn.

"How many American dollars (in Calabrese: *verdi americani*) did you give him?" asked the brother-in-law.

"A heavy load (*molto pesante*). But it was worth it."

"Will he want more?"

"Who knows with these mobsters? (*Come fai per sapere con questi Mafiosi?*)"

Long pause. Incomprehensible words shouted at Popescu from the room by a woman. Loud TV noise in the background.

"Is he gone, you're sure?" asks the brother-in-law.

"He's dead all right. That's all I care about. The fuck finally paid for what he did to me."

The telephone conversation, along with motive and the continuous threats Popescu uttered over the years against the Colonel, comprised the case against the Brooklyn grocer. By the time the case reached the court, Popescu had already been tried and convicted in the press. Kemeny could not win. Everyone was shocked when she rejected the plea of conspiracy to commit murder in the second degree and its 15-year sentence.

On the screen, the tall woman with a grave, musical voice, spoke about her defense strategy.

"The case rested on the telephone conversation, and on its translation from the Calabrese dialect into English. It therefore rested on the translator. If indeed the words had the meaning he gave them, the accused was compromised. If not, I could generate enough doubt in the jurors' minds to make them acquit.

"I had to shake his testimony somehow, and his credibility. But that was not easy. The translator, who became the prosecution's expert witness, was the most eminent expert in the field of Italian linguistics, author of several books on the subject and of the only dictionary of Southern Italian dialects to date. There was no point trying to belittle his knowledge of the language. So I decided to go about it in an unorthodox way."

On cue, the film of her cross examination of the expert witness started to roll.

Professor Anatol Della Croce was an unusually tall, dark man, large without being fat. His black cashmere blazer, burgundy silk ascot and crocodile attaché case betrayed an appetite for luxury he didn't bother to conceal.

"Professor Della Croce." Kay approached him, striding into the camera eye gracefully. It was winter and she wore a light wool maroon suit. The color made her eyes seem bigger, and the tailored cut of her skirt clothed her body well. "You are a most eminent expert in Italian linguistics."

His eyes twinkled when he answered.

"I am, Madame. Indeed."

"You have two doctorates, one from Harvard, one from Yale —" she proceeded to recite a litany of his accomplishments, pacing the room, her face a vivid mask of admiration.

"Your honor," the prosecutor interjected, unnerved, "we have already described Professor Della Croce's expertise on direct yesterday."

"I am doing nothing objectionable your honor, am I?"

"You're not, Ms. Kemeny. But I'm eager to hear you get to the point. Sometime before lunch."

She nodded.

"Professor. Are you absolutely certain that your translation of the exchange between the two brothers-in-law is accurate? Entirely accurate?" she asked, still from afar, looking alternately at the expert witness and the jury.

"Madame, I would not be testifying here if I weren't."

"How about this expression *verdi americani*. Could it mean anything else? Anything other than American dollars? Wouldn't American dollars be more like *dollari americani* or *soldi americani* or some other such wording, much more common when people refer to money?"

The Professor shifted his shoulders a notch, as if bothered by a sudden ache.

"I'm afraid that couldn't be. You see, the expression *verdi americani* is quite established as meaning American dollars in Italian. It appears in 27 dialects and in the standard colloquial language. It has become, over the past few decades, ever since the start of the greater Italian migration to America, alas, a linguistic certainty. And, though I profoundly disapprove of this bastardization of our language, the expression is, I'm afraid, here to stay."

"But if we took it literally — just bear with me for a moment, Professor, help me out here. If we took it literally, what would this expression mean?"

"My dear lady, there is no such thing as taking an expression literally."

"But word for word, even if incorrect, let's hear it, what would it mean?"

"Well you don't need a linguist to tell you that verdi is green in the plural. Greens. And, obviously, American."

"I see. So *verdi americani* would then, taken literally, mean American greens."

"It would, but it emphatically does not."

The Professor's face took on a look of silent dismay.

"And you are convinced, Professor, that average Italians in this part of the world have not adopted the expression American greens for a more literal purpose. Such as, well, the obvious. Greens. Vegetables. Lettuce, spinach, that sort of thing."

"I must say, Madame, your point is rather mystifying. Especially considering the context. I've never heard of such literal use for those words."

The young woman flashed a warm, elusive smile and moved closer to the witness. Her eyes stopped on him fleetingly, then went to the jury and remained there.

"You have been called a 'genius' of Italy's living languages by your contemporaries."

"Only by my fellow linguists. Ours is an unglamorous profession."

"Unglamorous? Not so, if you consider some of your travel articles. By the way, Professor, how do you travel?"

"How do you mean?"

"You know, coach, business class, first class?"

"I travel first class Madame. But I do not travel very often."

"Where, and how often?"

"Italy, usually, for the summer."

"Who do you socialize with, generally?"

"Well. Professors, like myself. A few enchanting ladies." He smiled widely.

"Would you be kind enough to read for the court this paragraph you wrote?"

Kemeny eased herself near him and handed him a well marked printed page. He placed his reading glasses low on the aquiline nose and read his own words with visible pleasure, in colorful baritone.

"That very evening the Count of Trino provided me with indubitable proof of his friendship. Acting in a mysterious fashion, he whisked me away in his Maserati to an elegant outdoor cafe in the Piazza di Spagna, where I had the honor of finding the prince of Montereale, still splendid in his twilight years, quietly sipping an aperitivo in majestic solitude."

"Thank you — thank you Professor. You may stop here."

The large shoulders fell forward slightly, disappointed. The Professor had trouble parting with his words.

"Would it be accurate to say, Sir, that you count mostly such aristocratic friends among your acquaintances?"

"Well, yes, I am myself as you might know of baronial origins, albeit from Turin."

"Albeit?'

"Well, there is a great deal of unrest among the Torinese and Venetian upper classes when it comes to establishing which is of superior descent. Venetians have been rather mixed. And then of course there are the Florentines who claim their origins are the purest. So far, history is on their side."

"Where do you live, Professor? Where in New York, I mean. Not the address, just the neighborhood, and the type of residence please."

"I have a penthouse on Fifth Avenue."

"Do you cook your own meals?"

The question mark on the Italian's face deepened.

"I'm afraid not, Madame. I favor eating out."

"So you never actually buy food — such as, groceries, say."

"No I do not."

"Do you ever go to Brooklyn, Professor?'

"Hardly."

"Do you ever count, say, a greengrocer, like the accused among your acquaintances?"

"I am sad to say I do not."

"How then, Professor, do you expect to know what *verdi americani* means today, in Brooklyn, to a Romanian greengrocer who uses his wife's Italian dialect which is by no means his mother tongue, who mixes English words, sometimes even Romanian words, who speaks, in other words, a language mix you've never even begun to encounter anywhere near your ivory tower on upper Fifth Avenue, and certainly not among your baronial friends?"

The Professor seemed dismayed.

"How can you expect us to believe that you're an expert in the Calabrese dialect as it is spoken in Brooklyn, New York, today, by the lower middle classes, when you yourself admit you never come in contact with them?"

She closed in on him, so close he instinctively withdrew further in his chair.

"Didn't you yourself say in your landmark book on Southern Italian dialects published in 1978, I quote: 'Dialects change periodically, perhaps as often as every decade. What's more, they take on an entirely new life in other countries where Italians settle, such as Canada or the United States. Dialects are all the more exceptional for changing so quickly, for their dizzying pace which puzzles the scientist and perpetually nourishes his mind.'?"

The courtroom was quiet. Kay's eyes were fixed on the jury, taking them with her for a wild ride with a hypothesis that suddenly didn't seem so farfetched.

"So isn't it possible, Professor, that the Romanian greengrocer simply gave a heavy load of vegetables — greens, from Florida, not Mexico or Chile for example, but American greens, to the owner of a local Italian restaurant who paid well, in cash, but took almost all of our grocer's supply? It was worth it, he says on the tape. Couldn't that mean he got good money for it, it was worth putting up with other customers' complaints for the day? And isn't it possible Professor that, since many Italians who own restaurants are called, jokingly and not so jokingly mobsters, and because the brother-in-law himself was no stranger to the subject, my client could have called his big customer by that name?

"Isn't it possible that the mention of the colonel's death in the same breath had no relation to the previous conversation? The TV was on in my client's house at the time of the call, and the news confirmed that the former Securitate colonel died in the hospital that day. He had been in a coma when he was found. The brother-in-law must have overheard the TV and naturally asked the question. 'Is he gone, you're sure?' Popescu naturally answered he felt revenged by the death."

The screen went blank for a moment and then Kemeny reappeared in an interview after the verdict, with court TV reporter Michael Marino.

"And so you won."

"Yes. The jury was out just three hours. My client went free."

"Was the murder ever solved?"

"No. Never. But that doesn't surprise me. The Colonel had many enemies."

"How did the Professor react, in the end?"

"He took me to dinner at Le Cirque and thanked me for opening his eyes to real life. He vowed to acquire an Italian cookbook, and have me over at his apartment for a tryout. I never mustered the courage to go."

Stone laughed. This woman was smart. Very smart.

Krone turned down the volume.

"There are a few things that are possible problems with her, Bob. She had abortions. And isn't married. All that you knew."

He knew. That was all right, that was precisely the point. She had to be different. Not gay, nor ill, nor disabled. That would have been too much. But different.

"She's not all-American," he said. "That's for sure. But she's not running for my job either. A touch exotic is fine for human rights."

It was Krone's turn to laugh.

Stone moved towards the screen. She was perfect. She captured her audience and they went along with her. That was just what he needed. A voice like Kemeny's. What he liked best about her was the disassociation from all parties, her neutral stance. Better yet, her opposition to all things socialist, the fact that she belonged to the so called "enlightened" right. He needed that just now to shatter this image they had of him, too pink for comfort.

But listening to her make her point in court he knew he'd have to work hard to get her. She was the real thing this one.

"All right Marvin. Bring her in."

* * *

Marvin Krone met Catherine Kemeny at the reception desk off the main lobby, wishing her well with requisite formality. They had met before.

"You look beautiful today, Ms. Kemeny."

Kay acknowledged the compliment with a slight smile.

That day, indeed, she felt beautiful. She had made it a point to be. It was high summer and even Capitol Hill's finest shed their outer layers, capitulating to the balmy weather, liberated by heat. In her slim tunic made of ivory silk and her skirt which rose just above the knee, Kay was cool, elegant, unstudied. She wore her thick mane of chestnut hair up, caught in a simple clip of matte gold, her only jewelry. Her beauty was serene, composed, despite the anxiety she had been fighting all morning, at the prospect of meeting the President.

"Thank you, Marvin," she said, gratefully.

"He has a few phone calls still. He might be a few minutes. I have to join him. Can I get you some coffee?"

"No, thank you."

"Water, perhaps?' Krone smiled again.

"Yes. Water, please."

She settled in a solitary chair, away from the other visitors, and tried to steady her breath. This was it then. This was the White House. And it was everything she had imagined. Tall, stately, imposing. She watched visitor after visitor rise and follow men in dark suits through doors that led to the presidential quarters.

Could this be happening, or was it still a dream?

It felt like a year, certainly not a week, since Senator Endicott flew to New York to give her the news in person. She was the number one candidate for the human rights post. All she had to do now was meet the president. That was all! "Everyone, including Millicent Stone, is behind this Kay," Ed assured her. "You have everything they're looking for. The background. The future. The clout with the press." She resisted at first, but Ed demolished every argument she made. He was so sure this was her calling. He was so happy to make her his political protégé.

The problem was that she had great reservations about Robert Stone's administration.

Kay touched her ivory shoulder bag and felt, in the outside pocket, the comforting shape of her minuscule silver icon, Saint Nicholas. The saint that bore her father's name. She held it tight between her fingers. No one was there to see her, so she crossed her heart quickly with a tiny motion, for good luck.

By the time Marvin Krone returned she felt ready. He took her through a long corridor to the Oval Office, briefing her on the way about what Robert Stone might want to hear and what she might want to find out.

"By the way —" he asked, just before opening the imposing door, beyond which the President waited.

"Will you be looking for him again, if you get this job?"

"Looking for who?" she asked calmly, unwilling to share her secret hope with anyone.

"The Inquisitor, of course. Grigor Vorody."

THREE

He learned early in life to talk about himself in the third person. Somehow the words "I", "me", hardly applied to his ever-shifting identity. He mastered the art of being everything to everyone by keeping his true self at great distance. But over the years, so many years, the self went the same way as the soul. It landed somewhere far away, perhaps on another planet, an alien being he now addressed as Grigor Vorody. He was a relic, wasn't he? Like Racklee, like Pavlov, like their slice of history.

Memories crowded him out of the large square of light where he had sat on the single chair in the empty room he called home. What right did he have to that light? He rose and paced angrily the darkened borders of shadow.

At first, after he defected from Hungary, he chose New York as his residence. He wanted a city where he could lose himself, where the outer noise could cover for a while the deafening hum within.

But then the woman found him.

He traveled for a time, seeking a spread out, end-of-the-road kind of place, a giant garage for transients who pulled in and parked there on their last stop. A final destination in the midst of the infinite freedom of the ocean. He found Miami.

And here he was. From every corner of this room, he saw water. He pulled a pair of green army binoculars from his belt and fixed his eyes against the cold lens. An ocean liner entered his viewpoint, growing steadily, until it finally filled the horizon.

He chose to live at the furthermost tip of an island. He found immediately just the place, it wasn't hard. No one wanted a house that fell prey to every strong wind. To enter it, it was either the swamp, the water, or a thin rope bridge tied to the island's last solitary tree. The house was yellow and gray like a lemon gone bad, set right on the water, holding on to a white patch of sand. Even in a minor storm, the kind that hit almost every day in rainy season, the entire structure shuddered and the windows broke. The floors cracked, ballooned, and traveled at least an inch at a time. The entire house shifted permanently, like its tenant.

The Inquisitor took the lens away from his eyes and held the binoculars to the side. The horizon regained its infinity. The ocean liner seemed little more than a speck now. Comparing to it, *Larissa*, which was moored less than ten feet away, seemed colossal. She rocked gently on the crest of each wave, sculpting columns of foam. One day soon the wind would tear her anchor out and the boat, the chair and the ruined house would all be on their way.

Some days were sunnier than others — the days without memories.

Today is dark. Misty. He is in his office at home, working since dawn on a report for his job at secret service in Hungary. He is only 30. He listens to Wagner and thinks of his father. Could he have known what his son's life would become when he made him his legacy?

He is the best they've ever had, and they know it. His superiors are impressed. He speaks English like an American and he can memorize two decks of cards at a glance. He's better than the older guys, even though he's just out of KGB academy. The chain of command from Moscow warned the Hungarians. This time they were getting more than they bargained for. They were getting a thinking man, a brilliant operative who could conceive strategy.

When he kills, he uses martial arts, because it's clean and easy. When he tortures, he gets results faster than the others. He plays with his victims' minds until they open up to him like clams in hot water. They come to him on a platter. When he's done, he feeds them to his lieutenants. He's made commander already. Father should be proud. His son steps through life light and dangerous as a panther. They are afraid of him, all of them. Unseen, unheard, he catches even the secret service by surprise.

At first his targets are local but in less than two years he is assigned foreign duties. He excels at them because he lived among the capitalists when he was a boy. He speaks their language and reads their minds. Most importantly, he is trusted. He is the son of Hungary's great communist hero, Sandor Vorody.

The order comes with a half empty cup of Russian tea and the breakfast cake Xenia makes for him every morning.

She is his lover and his maid. She has big breasts and large hips and she looks nothing like Mother.

"Pavlov wants to meet you," the note says in Russian. He has no time to shave. They are downstairs, just so he doesn't have time to let anyone know where he's heading. Why should that surprise him? "Lesson number three, comrade," he hears Liddy sing cheerfully into his ear. "Never trust anyone. Not even me."

Pavlov will have to see him with a day's growth and everyday shoes. The parade pair is out for repair. Xenia spits on the black leather and wipes it nervously with her elbow. Her breasts dangle and bounce, milky and soft, and he can't help it. He squeezes one until she rolls on her back, spreads her legs and purrs, like a fat cat. But there's no time for that. The comrades are outside the door. He is in uniform. He flies in a military plane with four other officers. Russians. He speaks with them about many things, nothing serious, just soldier talk to pass the time. They marvel at how fluent he is in Russian. "I was there four years. Training at Lubyanka. And my maid is Russian. Xenia." They laugh and elbow each other. One of them must have looked inside.

They make him wait all day in a dark steel chamber with hardly any air to breathe and just enough light to see his own shadow. It's late and he's hungry, thirsty and tired by the time they come for him. They take his weapons away, including the thin black pen he carries in his vest pocket. He uses it better than a knife. When he protests they say, "It's all right, tovarish, you don't need to write today."

He still has his fingers.

There's no other way to describe Pavlov's tomb than just that — a tomb. He spent four years here and he didn't know about the labyrinth they built under Lubyanka. Leave it to the Russians, he thinks, as they walk him through tunnel after tunnel. Leave it to the comrades to do a job like this underground.

Pavlov's tomb is cone shaped and tall. Like a pyramid, or a mausoleum. Light comes from somewhere, and it looks like bright daylight, but it's all packed into just one thin stream. It hits him right in the eyes. No matter which way he turns, the blinding ray follows.

Pavlov is in front of him but he can only tell the outline of his body. He is slight.

"I hear good things about you, Vorody. I hear you are a thinker."

"Sir, I am honored to serve you and the cause."

"Then listen carefully. I want to know what you think of this. I have a plan."

Pavlov tells him he wants him to get recruited by CIA.

"Find a way to get to them. You've heard they're as naive as children — don't count on it. Find a way to convince James Jesus Angleton. He is so good at spotting double agents that the Americans think he's paranoid.

"I'll arrange anything you need. I want this. Even if we have to hurt ourselves. I'll provide the sacrificial lambs. But you report only to me. Understand? Just me."

"What happens if you're unavailable?"

"Just ask for Pavlov. One of us is always here."

Later, when he becomes level one at KGB, more than five hundred feet into the ground below Lubyanka, he hears that Pavlov is not a man. He is an entity. Stalin invented him to breathe fear into his highest officers. The KGB chief who reigns well above presidents, prime ministers and party secretaries is an undying force, an absolute power, going by that name, always the same name. Pavlov. Indestructible.

"I have an idea I want to run by you, comrade Pavlov," he says just before he is helped out of the chair. His eyes hurt and he notices even when they're closed he can't chase the ray.

The contour raises its small arm to the right and the helpers disappear.

"I'm listening, commander Vorody."

"I want to set up a disinformation network in Hungary. I've been thinking about it for some time. You have one here and it services the east bloc well — but mine will be a little different."

"How?"

"You use media, mainly, to spread disinformation. Newspapers, TV —. I want to use people."

"Who?"

"Dissidents. Defectors. Turn them into pigeons. Messengers. They will not know they carry, which is why they'll do it reliably. We'll let them go, we'll give them the information as a slip up from a trusted friend, and they'll exchange it for political asylum in the West."

"What do you need from me?"

"The word. If you say yes, I'll run with this on my own. I need very little budget and few people. This is a controlled operation. And the pigeons get a passport instead of pay. It's all free, you see? I thought I'd call it H.M. The Human Ministry."

There is a long pause. A fly tears through the light beam above him. How did it get here? This cone ends somewhere outside.

"If I give you a bomb powerful enough, will you blow up the planet?" the contour asks, bending slightly to the left, reaching for something on his desk. The object is metal. It makes a scratchy noise on the steel surface.

Grigor jumps.

"Don't worry, it's just the tape recorder. I turned it off. There, you see?"

The question defies the arithmetic of the space around them.

"I can't see."

"All right then. Tell me. If I give you a bomb, will you blow up the planet?"

What does he want, he wonders, but instinct takes over and he answers,

"Yes. If you ask me."

Pavlov shuffles papers and rises. A chill passes through Grigor. The KGB chief is no bigger than a child. Could it be that this man is someone else, not Pavlov but some kind of dwarf, some test, some deadly surprise, some other Russian oddity?

"You got it, Vorody," the midget says and hands him a page he can't see. It smells of glue and ink. It feels a little wet. He touches it and folds it, for later.

"You got your disinformation ministry."

FOUR

"So, what do you think?" the President asked Kay after she settled in.

"How do I look? Compared to TV and the photos you've seen? Disappointed?"

"No," she answered plainly. Circumspect.

"Come on, be candid. I'll tell you what I think about you."

He turned sharply, with an agility that surprised her, like everything else about this meeting.

"You are beautiful." He no longer smiled. His face had turned serious, impenetrable. "You are too beautiful."

He studied her reaction.

"Thank you." No blushing, no panic, no inflection in her voice. As if nothing could take her by surprise. "But I will point out this is a discriminatory remark."

He broke into a wide smile.

"Got me!" he said, looking relieved, as if he had just found a new friend. "Still, I wish you told me I was too handsome to be President."

"OK, you are."

His smile came through his eyes with the power of midday sun, intoxicating. Then, without warning, his face grew serious again.

"Listen, I am as nervous as you are. Why don't we have a drink."

He rang for lemonade without leaving her eyes for a moment. He watched her drink it in silence, and poured her another, casually, as he would for a friend. She could hear the faint sound of Mozart playing in a room nearby. The curtains moved gently in the breeze of the air conditioning, and from where she sat she could see the roses wilting, begging for a rainy day.

She began to relax. Suddenly she felt at home near this man, as if she had known him before. The Oval Office was just a room where she was spending a summer afternoon, and the President a man she had met in another life.

He spoke softly, gesturing often with his hands. She didn't think a man could have such beautiful hands.

"This country needs someone like you but it also needs someone like me. We don't see things the same way. You're born behind the Iron Curtain, to an intellectual family and a stately home. I'm from East Toledo, with poverty written all over my face. You saw your father jailed and then killed because he wrote about the truth. I never met my father. You come from a totalitarian state and you're scared to death that if we give the government too much power it'll be the same communist nightmare by a different name all over again. You want total freedom. You want everyone to fend for himself. You are afraid of the state. You want the right to find your own way. You want choices. You want a better world.

That's what we have in common. That's what we have to work with. And it's a lot, believe me. A whole lot. The important thing is that we both go for the same goal. Hand in hand we can find social justice, which is what I am all about. I just go about it my way."

He rose and stood by the window, his head surrounded by a million particles of daylight, like a crown.

"I don't believe it's a jungle out there. I don't want to hear about the lion's share and survival of the fittest, and all that gladiator right wing stuff."

His eyes fixed her like she was a target.

"Not in my country."

He came closer, so close she could smell the rose garden on him. Any closer and she'd be brushing his hands.

"Maybe I'm wrong, I'd like to hear what you think. I want honesty. I want you to call me names, if that's what you have to do, but when this is done, when you leave this room, you and I are on the same side. I want you to know about me, fight with me. I want you to interview me for this post. In the end, I want to be worthy of you. Because your job will be more important than mine. In the long run, you will have much more power over how people are treated in this country than I ever could. I'll be dead long before you are. If a gunshot or this heart of mine doesn't kill me, the press will. The voters will. Or just simply time. You are what I leave behind. My legacy, human rights. Ask me everything you want to know. I have all the time in the world."

Kay had never experienced such charisma. She was not prepared for this intriguing blend of strength and weakness, and the extraordinary effect it had when it came right at you. Stone was a master manipulator, yet she had never heard a more sincere ring, a more vibrant truth in anyone's voice. He had a warmth, a concern for the world that had to be fabricated, yet he radiated a kind of personal heat that could only be genuine. Power suited him precisely because he played it down with such grace and honesty. Yet every moment you spent around him you knew, you could never forget, that he was President.

She understood now how he rescued that 10-year-old Israeli child from the May 1972 PLO bombing in Paris. She could still see the picture that ran everywhere during his presidential campaign, young Bob Stone holding the girl in his arms against the backdrop of the devastated building. He really seemed capable of braving fire and terrorists. He really was the American Hero.

How had qualities so rare and precious come together in this rather portly man from Toledo? He had the glow of a diamond in the rough who by some kind of personal magic had settled comfortably as the jewel in his country's crown. His portliness was indulgent, thus human. It worked for him, like everything else. He was tall and well built, a big man more than anything. His strong belly, well disguised in a black suit and crisp white shirt which he kept casually opened at the neck, somehow complimented him, made him seem earthy, familiar. Wasn't it just like Bob Stone to turn his faults into assets? To make the most of what he didn't have and use what he did have to the fullest?

She decided that anyone who could make that kind of speech to win her over deserved a fair chance. Besides, she had nothing to lose. She interrogated him, asking him everything she wanted to know and never dreamt she could. She was honest with a man who could, if he chose to, be dishonest to the extreme. He was superb the entire time.

He described his most ambitious thoughts, told her things he knew she'd hate — more welfare, more taxes, more government spending, more money and allowances to pressure groups, more control, more bureaucracy to manage the control. He didn't once try to persuade her he was right. He just told her his truth. It all just had to be done this way. And at almost every turn she found him to be right. She agreed with him though he never asked for her approval.

"You're telling me too much — aren't you manipulating me?" she tested him.

"You bet I am," he replied. "How else can I bring you to me, how else can I convince you to give me a chance? I need you. May I call you Kay?"

"You may."

She called him Mr. President even though he asked her twice to use his first name. She held on to this distance, the very last barricade. Ed was right about this meeting. Her perspective of Stone had begun to change.

Kay knew their time was up when he brought up again the few personal things he probably always used in closing to warm his good-byes. She watched him run through the motions of his finale with serious eyes which suddenly didn't match the rest of his face. He spoke the words he always used when he moved on, the words that didn't mean anything anymore. And, as he was winding down his act, the man before her became a stranger.

Kay felt a pang of sorrow. She wanted him back. But he was gone. His eyes were elsewhere, as was his mind, galaxies away in a place where she found herself wishing she could travel with him.

But she could not. The President who swore to lock himself away with her for eternity had only scheduled two hours of his time.

* * *

Kay left the White House completely dazed. How could she have foreseen what just happened? How could she have predicted the affinity she felt for a man whom, until that afternoon, she had so profoundly mistrusted?

She went straight to her hotel, with the distinct feeling that she was being followed. It was that old communist paranoia, she suspected, as she passed again the young couple who had been there, on that same bench when she left in the early afternoon. It was not until she closed the thick drapes at the Regency Excelsior that she felt safe again.

She called Ed and left him one brief message.

"I'm in."

* * *

By 7 pm President Stone had finished everything on his agenda, including the briefing with Krone and the communications staff regarding next morning's press conference at which he would announce the nomination of Catherine Kemeny for Human Rights Chief.

He had gone out on a limb with her, telling her much more than he told any other nominees.

He dialed a number that was not coded, and heard the telephone at the other end ring for awhile. Finally a voice, bubbly and unmistakable, chirped:

"Hello!"

"I'm sorry, sweetheart, but I have to cancel tonight."

"Bad boy," she breathed into the phone. "Tell me why."

"Big trouble with Saddam."

"And tomorrow, sugar?"

"Yes. Tomorrow is fine."

The fact was, even though the meeting with Catherine Kemeny left him energized, he just wasn't in a mood today for the Texas blonde. Good old Saddam, it worked every time.

With Millicent gone and his mistress postponed, he was a free man for the night. He leaned back in his giant leather swivel, touched a button and shut out what was left of the light. Music poured in, soothing, perfect, relaxing him, putting everything else out of his mind. Ella Fitzgerald. He snoozed in a half-conscious sleep.

He didn't sleep much better in his own bed, not since he became president. Or was it since George was born and everything changed? He couldn't remember exactly.

George arrived six years before at dawn at Toledo Hospital, and three doctors saw to it that the governor's wife had the hardest delivery money can buy.

"Where were you? They almost killed me —" Millicent searched for his hand after she woke up from deep sedation, her larynx still pounding from the tubes that had been forced into her lungs.

She was huge, still. He had expected her to deflate somehow, like a balloon. But then what did he know? He was the last born so this was really the first time he had to deal with pregnancy. Where his wife's belly had been there was an uneven hill, atop which lay two shapeless growths, attached to a plastic pump which was extracting droplets of an unidentified liquid. All he once praised, her lean limbs, narrow waist and delicate high breasts, the clean, aristocratic line of her chin and the chiseled cheeks of the woman their Harvard colleagues used to call "Bob's medal," had yielded to the unknown forces of motherhood.

On the wall above her head, a map of the reproductive system exposed secrets about his wife's insides he did not wish revealed.

"You're all right now, Mill. I was out of town a day longer than I thought. I'm sorry. But the cesarean went well. It will just take a few days to heal. George is —." He paused, searching for a word that would capture the awkwardness of his joy. "He's so — big. Seven pounds."

Her eyes swelled with a wave of unexpected tears.

"Was she with you?"

"Who?"

"Your P.R. woman."

"Of course she was. Why shouldn't she be?"

His hand was firmly in hers now and for a moment he wondered, absurdly, if there was any way she could somehow feel Esther on his fingers.

"Did you see the baby?" he asked, hoping to distract her.

"No."

"Well — that's not — Nurse! Nurse!" he started for the door, grateful there was something about this that he could control.

"Bob, stop." Her voice was weak. "I don't want to see him yet. They've hurt me too much."

"They?"

"All of them. George. The doctors. You."

She buried her head into the pillow, away from him. Tears soaked her left cheek. Her face seemed congested, her features distorted, swollen. Her hair, always groomed and dyed a discreet ash blond, had thick dark roots and her aquiline nose ran. He handed her a Kleenex, realizing too late that she was too weak to use it. Reluctantly, he wiped a face he couldn't recognize.

A nurse rushed in.

"She has a high fever. This is no time to visit, Governor. You understand."

She changed the IV pouch and removed the breast pump with amazing dexterity. He stood up, relieved. He kissed Millicent on the forehead and took with him a startling taste of rubbing alcohol, sweat, and peppermint.

How did she find out about Esther?

He'd never know.

She never asked for a divorce. In time, he hoped she'd forget — or forgive. For the first year, her excuse was the baby. She couldn't sleep with him because George was colicky, then teethed, and always, each night, needed her in his room. Later the giant conjugal bed became too small to house the distance between them. He agreed, without much of a fight, to a separate bedroom.

"Darn," the President said waking abruptly, his mouth bitter with anguish. Ella's song was long over and the naked silence corrupted the evening with an unusual sadness.

"Better not sleep, if it's going to end this way."

FIVE

The phone rang at nine as Kay sat in her hotel room trying to write the speech for tomorrow's press conference.

"Give 'em a straight paragraph of flattered acceptance. It's what everyone does, suck up," Ed advised.

"I don't know," she replied. "That isn't my style at all."

"Come on Kay, You must have prepared something before today."

"Well, no. I never really believed Stone would accept a thorn like me in his crown."

The phone kept ringing and she was in no mood to answer. It might be Tony or her mother. She didn't have the strength to call either of them after she returned to the hotel, her temporary home. Let Mother and Tony see her tomorrow on the morning news. She'll call them after her acceptance speech. It was more dramatic that way. And safer.

"Do not breathe a word to anyone before the news conference," Krone had warned her.

And what could she tell them anyway, she reasoned. That she had succeeded or that she had succumbed? She thought of her father. The words Nicholas wrote in one of his journals: "I keep trying to tell myself that there is such a thing as good or bad, black or white, true or false, that the world, after all, is not all gray." She remembered watching him line up those words on paper like soldiers in the only war he knew how to fight.

"You're just like him, Kay," Ed told her when she kept saying no this trip, to politics, to this adventure in compromise. "You doubt everything, question everything. Sometimes I think you'd be better off relaxing a bit. Believing a little more in people. How about taking one thing a month at face value for a change? Do it as an exercise. Do it for me?"

She wished she could. But no one seemed to understand what it was like to live with her memories. Memories of her childhood, of what communism had done to her family. Memories of Grigor Vorody.

"This is Kay Kemeny," she finally answered, putting an end to the exasperating ring.

"Hey princess. How's your day? Mine sucks."

It was Tony.

"It's hot," she answered, distracted. "The flight here was fine. But it's hot as hell outside. And I have a four poster bed. You wouldn't believe the furniture in this place."

"Relax honey. You won't be there long. Which is just fine because I need you here. I'm having trouble with my still life, they won't accept it at that fucking show unless I pay for it. What am I supposed to do, sell my body for art?"

"I only left this morning, remember?"

"OK, I admit it, I'm lost without you. And my painting suffers. It's all too blue. What's up?"

The sound of his voice exhausted her. She yearned to say good-bye.

"Nothing much."

"The nomination fall through yet?"

"No."

"Talk to me, then. How did it go?"

"Can't say. Watch it tomorrow morning on the news."

Static suddenly came on the line.

"Hello? Tony? You're still there?"

More static.

"I don't think I could ever live with you in Washington with all those political fakes," he snapped.

"Don't worry. Washington is only an hour away".

"So tell me about him. The Prez. How is he in real life?"

She was silent.

"What's the matter, did the CIA put a wire on your phone?"

"Maybe. But it's not that."

"So then?"

It was crazy, she knew, but she felt she was betraying Stone when she spoke.

"I can't say much. He's definitely a puzzle. He's fascinating, and yet, he's just a man. Just a man, not a concept, or an institution. Or a fraud. Nothing like what I expected anyway."

Tony's silent resentment reverberated loudly into the phone, reminding Kay of the night before, when he dropped her off at LaGuardia. "Soon you won't need a ride," he'd said picking at a small tear in the black seat of her Mercedes. "They'll send you on the presidential jet."

"Don't be angry," as she hugged him, "I'll be back."

Now there was a quiver in his voice.

"I love you Kay. That's the only problem. You know that."

"I love you too," she lied.

* * *

"OK honey what now?" she snapped when the phone rang again. This time she was in bed with the lights off.

"We're getting friendlier all the time." The voice startled her. She thought it might come out of a dream — she must have fallen asleep. "Who is this?"

"Your new friend. The one you met in an egg-shaped room this afternoon."

She jumped up, her arms instinctively wrapped around her half naked body. My God. It was Stone. The clock said 1 am.

"I do a lot of work at night — I get a second wind. How about you?'

"I don't sleep very much myself but this time I confess I was in bed. The travel, the pressure, all that."

"You wrote your flattered speech?"

"I jotted down some notes over dinner. Literally over dinner. There's salad dressing on every page."

She wouldn't give him the satisfaction of admitting that she had been poring over the speech for most of the evening.

"They'll do. If I know you."

"Oh but you don't." She felt bold. She was bold. It was not clear to her how familiar she could be. He was the President after all, even if nothing he had done since she first laid eyes on him was remotely what she expected.

"I want to see you tonight."

"It's late and I'm in bed."

"Please." His voice was light. "I have something we didn't discuss and it might come up at the press conference tomorrow. Not the end of the world but worth a chat."

"OK, but where?"

"I'll come by your hotel, if you don't mind. We can talk in your living room. I know a way to get in without fuss. I'm bringing up only one guard. Half-hour OK?"

What do you wear when the President comes to your hotel suite in the middle of the night? A suit? A dress? A robe? She laughed. It was a funny way to have her second meeting with the most powerful man in the world. She settled for a long sleeveless summer dress, as tan as her skin, something she would wear if she entertained a casual guest. No point in being formal. The President didn't strike her as a formal man. Was she too bare? The shoulder straps hung loosely and one of them constantly fell. So what?

She was right, the President was not formal. He came in boyish and cool in jeans and a white shirt opened three buttons down. The skin on his chest was rugged. Dark.

He had a hard-eyed man behind him whose suit jacket stuck out at stiff angles. There must have been a small army of them downstairs. He sent for food even before he said hello. "I'll have a burger, how about you," he smiled.

"I'll have the same." Suddenly she was hungry again.

"You have this strange quality, you know?" she told him later, as she looked over his shoulder, reading the words he had written about her in his nomination speech. "You come in and it's a new day, a new hunger, a new reason to be awake. How do you ever sleep?"

He was relaxed, leaning feet up on the giant sofa opposite hers, a sea of papers settled comfortably on his belly, like a pasha and his harem of thoughts. His face glistened in the semi darkness, the deep blue of his eyes eerie, bizarre — he didn't want much light, "just enough to read and to look at you."

"I sleep alone." He paused and his eyes tore her face apart. Then he stopped.

"It's not what you asked. I sleep here and there, 10 minute naps, and about 4 hours each night. Survival sleep. I slept better when I was Governor, that's for sure. And you?"

She had absolutely no control over the words she spoke.

"I sleep alone too."

The knock on the door and the burgers came as a welcome distraction. But she knew that things would never be simple between them again. They ate and talked, passing papers and ketchup. A blood-like stain spread on the first page of his nomination announcement, and they laughed.

She had never met anyone so completely in lust with life. The broad smile betrayed not a trace of fatigue, the passion with which he spoke never dwindled, the abandon with which he bit into his food never subsided.

"Nothing like a burger at midnight, I don't care if I'm never skinny again!"

And then there was the way he looked at her.

Out of the blue, he said,

"I'm having a good time, Kay. I'm having a great time.'

She didn't know what to answer. So she sat silently beside him, and looked him in the eyes. A current of air flew between them, like a bird. It fluttered, then stopped on his pages, lifting one and bringing it near her on the sofa. They both reached out for it at the same time. Their hands touched.

Her skin was like that flutter. Cool and smooth. And unattainable. Maybe she was too tall and fragile for him, maybe too smart. But Stone had never been that close to someone like Kay before.

He suddenly felt awkward. Intimidated. He felt an urge to touch her, to probe her, like an oddity. He wanted to learn more about her neck, how it felt to hold it. Long, graceful, vulnerable. About the consistency of her hair, how it could feel against the palm of his hand. Thick and fragrant. About that scar she had earned somehow. How? Whatever it was that scarred her, he wanted to make sure it never happened again. How did she manage in such a short time to make him yearn to breathe the air around her, to make him want to protect her?

They said good night well after 3 am. He rose to leave unwillingly. The press conference was scheduled for 9, and at 7 am he had summoned everyone to get a decision on Russia before 10 when he had Gordon in to deal with Saddam.

"Go on, Mr. President," she said at last, stretching her tall body as she rose to meet his hand. "I'll let you get your beauty sleep."

He laughed.

He held her hand one second longer than usual, and she gave him a quick kiss on the cheek.

"I forgot to tell you," she winked, opening the door for him. "Thanks for everything."

He pulled her towards him forcefully, roughly, shocking her, gripping her tightly, bringing her face to his, feeling her body through her dress, her waist, her belly, her hips. He was much too strong to resist. Her lips opened like a gift.

But he didn't take them. He released her carefully, slowly, and then caressed her hair, strand by strand, his eyes burning on hers, devouring her.

"We can't do this, Kay," he whispered. "We can't do this."

* * *

The next day, in the glow of cameras and the maze of known and famous faces — Millicent Stone, Marvin Krone, Larry and Kimberly Devane — Kay thanked the president for the nomination.

"We are fortunate in this country to have the freedom to elect a president who, by creating this post, fulfills the aspirations of millions. And I thank him on behalf of us all, on behalf of the entire free world. Once human rights are vested, ladies and gentlemen, they can never be denied."

She paused, suddenly overcome by emotion. This sunny day, this fragrant garden, the wings of a small bird fluttering above her head, perhaps a nightingale, her voice amplified by the powerful microphones, the admiring faces of the people around. Look at me, daddy, she murmured to the sky, look at me now.

Her voice came back firmly, stronger than before.

"There is a reason for everything in one's life, just as there is a reason for everything in history. I left my country of birth at the age of 12, crawling through mines and gunfire over the Hungarian border into freedom, after a dictatorial regime took away my rights and my father's life."

Kimberly Devane wiped her eyes and sighed, "Oh my God, honey, I didn't know it was so bad over there. You poor child." Her husband hushed her gently, patiently. "It's all right, sweetheart. It's all right."

Millicent Stone frowned.

* * *

"This wasn't supposed to be a rainy day, boys and girls. Just blasting sunshine, remember? It's not like we didn't give a good thought to tomorrow. It's not like we didn't put anything in the bank. Let's use it. Now's the time, children, let's do it right."

Clancy Leduc was a French import from New Orleans with a gene straight out of Napoleon, who shunned modern day comforts — air conditioning, ball-point pens, sleeping past dawn. He normally held his morning briefings at 7 am, despite his inclination to ask his staff to keep him company from the minute he left his private quarters. Where were the days when you could have them sleeping on cots in your chambers?

"Wake up, girls," he shouted.

"Wake up."

Leduc talked to his subordinates in his own special cadence. It wasn't exactly like the army, it was worse. The President's campaign manager and first senior advisor was a feared man. Not just because he had won a tough election for Stone, but because he had tremendous power over Millicent Stone, His number one ally.

"We've got problems with the religious right, Sir. Senator Moses. He called Kemeny a baby killer on the 10 o'clock news last night. We did the best we could to keep it until then. He was on line for 6 pm. They have a problem with her not being married. Before you know it we'll hear she's the antichrist," began one of the four assistants.

"The Deacon is acting up again. We expected that," Leduc whistled through the space between his front teeth. He only did that when he was angry. When things didn't go as he planned. "He picks up on the abortions. The s-s-status." He stood silent for a moment before the small battalion. He fixed his eyes on the wall of books that constituted the only decoration in his office. Leduc shunned distractions. His window oversaw the dark courtyard square he shared with the library. He looked up at his aides again. The lisp would stop now. He would make it stop. "But there's still an overwhelming majority there who will relate — women. Most of them will go with her all the way."

"Possibly, but maybe not. Certainly not the radical feminists," interfered the small voice of a pretty blonde.

"Nonsense," Leduc thundered. "They should be the first to applaud." His ears stuck out from the small, short-cropped head, like two antennae.

"We have a petition here from Florence Glaser, the Feminist Power advocate," the young woman spoke, now more confidently, handing her boss a thick file, and keeping a page for herself.

"Apparently Kemeny reviewed one of her books in the past. For the *Times*. Not good."

"Ouch," moaned a black aide, prim in his Ivy League navies. Leduc's eyes darted at him, but immediately went back to the blonde, as if he were holding her responsible for Kemeny's words.

"Can we control the damage now?"

"I don't know, Sir. There are leaflets flying about Washington since yesterday morning. 'FEMINISTS AGAINST THE KEMENY NOMINATION.'"

He looked around.

"So, girls, things haven't gone quite as we planned them, have they?"

"Sir," said the black aide. "There's something else."

"What?"

"Gay activists, especially the AIDS group."

"What about them?"

"They want her out too. There are 45 faxes here, and they assure us there will be more if we don't withdraw Kemeny. They're offended that she's a healthy, heterosexual woman. Their beef is that gays, especially HIV positive gays, are more in need of human rights legislation. They expected Geoffrey Chancellor to be nominated. They must have heard he made the short list."

"So who's the public going to relate to? Them or her?"

"Her — obviously," the acolyte answered, precipitously. "Except for some arts crowd and a piece of Hollywood. Maybe New York? But we all know, this country is bigger than that."

"You're wrong. The actors will stick by the President. It was his call, and they'll respect that. The AIDS group's already against him."

"Didn't she have a gay uncle?" the aide questioned, pulling some notes from his breast pocket. They were in a classic leather holder, matching his belt and his Gucci moccasins. "What did he die of? I know he was still young."

Leduc lit up.

"He was a ballet dancer. Everyone dig on this right now. If it was AIDS, we've got to run with it all the way to the polls."

Leduc's secretary breezed past them with a tray of messages and a cup of espresso. Leduc took an appreciative sip of the black muddy liquid, then let out a sigh. The day was truly about to start.

"Anything else?"

"So far that's it," spoke the fourth aide, the oldest of the lot. He looked exhausted. He wore a dark, frumpy suit and a red knit tie with the wrong knot. "Unless you want to look into this chase she'd been involved in, for that former KGB chief.

Leduc stood silent for a moment, computing the possibilities.

"She won't find him."

The aide frowned but went on, handing his boss a stack of freshly typed pages.

"The first news reactions so far, and the two victim cases we talked about. It's all there."

"All right, Lester." Leduc eyed him intensely. "Stay with me and let's review this. We'll call Sally Carmen from here. I'll place this story with her personally.

The rest of you are dismissed for now. Remember girls, six weeks to show time. Confirmation hearing is the Tuesday after Labor Day."

"Sir" — the blonde asked, as everyone was leaving, "You could perhaps ask the First Lady to arrange something favorable for this nominee, to bring in the feminist vote?"

Leduc eyed the young woman coldly.

"When I was you age, Candace, I thought before I spoke. Always. Don't disappoint me."

"Yes Sir. Forgive me."

"The First Lady will not be attached to any of this until Congressional acceptance is secured. Only then will she get behind Kemeny."

* * *

"Clancy, what the hell is going on here? I'm on the phone with the black caucus, with the congressman from San Francisco, with Menendez at the New York school board — is there anyone this nomination hasn't antagonized yet? Because if there is, I'd like to hear it." The President's anger was muffled somewhat by the speaker phone.

Leduc waved Lester out.

"It's under control, Bob. I can't tell you anything about the timing yet. But I haven't heard a thing about the black caucus or the school board."

"Well, no wonder pal. They came straight to me, and Devane let them."

"Who?"

"Reverend Pearson."

"What's their objection?"

"She's white, and a foreigner. You know...who's more American here, who's more in need. Says we're causing 'rage' among black activists who feel left out."

"What did you say?"

"I told him they shouldn't discriminate against her just because she's not one of them, how she suffered under communism. Then I passed him on to Krone who faxed him the whole press release."

"And?"

"He called back and said, 'Well OK, but we'll fight you all the way the first mistake she makes.'"

"I wouldn't worry too much about the reverend. Black reaction's been good overall. I think we're covered. Now, tell me about the school board."

"She got caught between them and the PTA over teaching kids about lesbian mommies."

"What did she do?"

"Threw them both out of her office and sent them home to read the Constitution."

Leduc chuckled.

"Did you hear the latest on Saddam?" Stone asked.

"No. What?"

"Gordon was here yesterday and we reviewed the evidence. Saddam claims we shot down our own plane."

Suddenly, a sharp noise came through the speaker, as if someone was smashing things in the oval office. Did I say something wrong, Leduc wondered, his glistening forehead folding like an accordion. Stone cursed right into the phone.

"Sorry. I dropped this model plane the Air Force gave me. I've been trying to figure this bombing thing. Damn. Now it broke."

"Well, things could be worse, couldn't they? I mean with Kemeny."

"Could they?" Stone asked, sounding focused again.

"It's troublesome but she's got a lot going for her. Middle America's crazy about her."

"True. I also have support from the moderate right. And our democrats are hanging in there nicely. We've got to give them a good angle soon. Are you working on it with the press?"

"I'm onto something with Sally Carmen. Two refugees in California, KGB torture victims from eastern Europe, how she saved them. The dignity angle."

"They'll thank me on the air for nominating her?"

"Not just them. Their families too. Both are married to Americans and have American children by now. We've got it all worked out, on FBC at 7 pm tonight, prime time."

Just then the presidential direct two rang.

"Hello — who?"

Leduc arched his brows, waiting to hear the answer through the speaker.

"Florence Glaser? Tell her to hold. See what I mean Clancy? Why the hell do I have to handle this? Maybe I should get Millicent involved here."

"I don't think so Bob. I'll take care of Florence. Put her through to me."

* * *

Kay's e-mail cursor was blinking furiously when she got back to the hotel. She was having dinner with Ed Endicott in one hour, to look at the first 24-hour reaction report to her nomination. She pressed the key to start messages. There were four, and they could certainly wait until she showered. The day had been hectic and exciting. She needed a drink.

She turned up the air conditioning, phoned for wine and opened her briefcase on the bed. She could see the first message screaming at her from the screen.

"Watch FBC at 7 pm, Sally Carmen. Dinner moved to 8:30 at Morton's, Ed." She looked at the gold framed clock above the fireplace. She still had 45 minutes. What was this about? Had Sally already whipped together a special on her? In less than two days?

She pressed Enter and watched the words disappear and the second message line up. A long list.

"Your agenda for tomorrow:

8 am Leduc's office re: strategy

9 am Larry Devane

10 am —"

The knock on the door stopped her just in time. She needed a cool drink and some distance before she could deal with Krone's tomorrow. She pressed Save, Next and opened the door.

When she was alone again, she took a sip of white wine and started to undress. She peeled off her linen jacket, then her short-sleeved dress. She started toward the shower. On the way, she glanced one more time at the screen.

On it there was the third message.

She stopped, her heart racing madly, her naked body drenched in cold sweat.

Why did he come to haunt her again?

The message wasn't signed, and nothing indicated the sender's code number. It was typed in bold capitals in a bookish, old font. It said:

"IF YOU STILL WANT THE INQUISITOR, CHECK HIS FATHER, SANDOR VORODY."

SIX

"Come on angel, faster, faster, no, don't, don't stop, rock me sugar, rock me all the way —." The rolling hills and valleys of Kimberly's sweet Southern tongue worked their usual magic, giving Bob Stone the electrical jolt of pleasure he'd been waiting for. He squeezed her soft, large breasts, watching bliss lift them higher and higher as she rode above him, ready to come, her arms stretched wide like the wings of a blonde cherub perched above the fountain of youth.

"Angel," Kimberly purred, content, in her breathless drawl, "this was one of the best we've ever had, good as peaches, like the one on the campaign bus in Illinois."

"You were eating donuts and me at the same time," Stone smiled, spent, making a mental note to warn Endicott whom he was meeting in ten minutes about Glaser and the feminist problem.

She laughed and rolled over him, her familiar weight suddenly unbearable in the summer heat.

He got up abruptly and, with his usual agility, was fully dressed before Kimberly had a chance to try and stop him.

"I'm out till next week, honey. I've got too much going with the human rights nominee."

"All right, angel." Her voice sang softly. "Meet you next Tuesday?"

The door clicked sharply behind him, before she could hear his good-bye.

Kimberly stayed behind, dreamy, cuddling the pillow that still smelled of her lover. A strand of graying hair, left on the edge of the fine embroidery was all he had left behind. She picked it and buried it between her breasts, opening with her fingers an invisible locket.

Another week without him. Another week with Larry.

She sighed, and straightened a rebel lash caught in a tear drop. Suddenly she felt so tired, so weary. Her arms, like lead, moved slowly, painfully, to her purse. One pill, two, make it three. Before long, she was perky, dressed and ready.

* * *

Endicott was five minutes late and apologized for another five.

Stone handed the Senator Leduc's report, and briefed him on his concerns about the pressure groups. It was clear they were trying to jeopardize Kay Kemeny's nomination.

"Don't give the media the whole picture. Accomplishments, successful trials, you know, all gradual, and a big splash at the end. Every time they get nasty, kill it with a good deed.

"Plant a few negatives and let her break their hearts when she speaks in her own defense. She's had abortions — open the debate on it from your side."

He wasn't sure everything was getting through to Endicott. He wasn't sure he was the best man for the job.

Why the hell did she insist on picking him?

* * *

If there ever were a time when Ed wanted to come out, it was after the inauguration when Stone addressed the Senate on homosexuality.

"Some things are worth fighting for," he remembered Stone saying. "Gay bashing, discrimination, lack of acceptance, lack of equality, that's something I vowed to fight against and you know that I'm committed to that. But I need everyone's help. Everyone who cares about human rights."

But Ed couldn't do it. He couldn't come out.

He apologized to the President in private. He rambled about the consequences to his life. His political allies, his community, his career. How misplaced and awkward he would feel, how shattered his family would be. He wished he could have done it. He wanted so much to be worthy of Stone.

But he'd be worthy now. He'd protect Kay Kemeny.

* * *

Langley, Virginia

The gun-metal door bore no sign. Jim Lennox shifted his Styrofoam coffee cup to his left hand, punched in the code and entered the windowless conference room.

"Good morning, Sir," his assistants said in perfect synchrony. Only Beatrice remained silent, standing. "You're early today."

He did not reply. He was early every day. Which made them late, always late. They were supposed to start work an hour before him, at 7 am sharp. But there was still steam rising from their coffee cups.

"I'll need a moment alone with Beatrice."

He pulled his chair to the narrow end of the acid green metal table, leaving a fresh trail on the linoleum floor. Federal standard gray and 10 years old. Why would he expect anything to change here? The place still looked like the storage area it had been before the CIA converted it to offices. And why should he expect any more for Domestic Containment, a division that officially didn't even exist?

"You're off the books, Jim." Carson has warned him when he first started. "Containment is our illicit child. We cannot put it on the family tree yet. But we will someday, you'll see."

Ten years later Lennox was still waiting for legitimacy.

"Beatrice," he summoned his female lieutenant. "Get me a napkin, will you sweetheart. And then let's hear the good news."

Beatrice looked different this morning. Behind the dusty crust of make up her face was flushed. She put the napkin down and stood there, awaiting his command.

He set his cup carefully on the beige square and gestured her to start.

"Sir, I have some information that could give Containment a permanent seat on Seven."

She sat and he watched her legs cross gracefully, showing a glimpse of white lace, unexpected under the dowdy dress. This morning Beatrice was not just different, she was downright foxy.

Lennox smiled.

"A seat on Seven? You're going to put me at the daily meeting of the deputy directors? Bea, talk to me."

"It happened last night," she started, animated, pulling her chair closer to his. "Last night Graveyard wrapped up the routine check on Catherine Kemeny. She's the woman the President just nominated —"

"I know. I read all about it."

"They ran the usual on her, you know, family —"

"Cut to the chase, Bea, I know the drill."

"And the surveillance report we've gathered since her name surfaced on the White House short list."

Lennox tapped his foot impatiently.

"It seems that one of our researchers followed a hunch. He noticed that Kemeny pursued several cases in the past five years, all related to this one Eastern European man. Some torturer. So my kid called up our friends at Justice to get the word on her. It turns out Kemeny is obsessed with this guy. She even got reprimanded twice for pushing the wrong buttons at FBI."

"So who's the man? Some private vendetta?"

"That's just it, boss. It's more serious than that." Beatrice's voice was now victorious.

"He's a big shot. The biggest in Budapest. And level one in Moscow too. He was the Secret Service Chief and KGB Commander for Hungary."

Lennox grabbed her file.

"Let me see."

He looked it over carefully. Of course, the report stopped with the bare facts. His division was not allowed to analyze or conclude. But this case was different. The researcher had overstepped his authority and called Justice.

"Did you tell anyone upstairs?" he asked Beatrice, who was leaning over his shoulder now, reading along with him. Her breasts almost touched his back. A whiff of her familiar perfume reached his nostrils.

"Not yet, Jim" she spoke this time softly, very close to his ear. "I wanted you to be the first."

* * *

Kay opened the thick brown envelope she received from her New York office. It was filled with yellowed papers she acquired over the past five years. Some were as old as her high school days. In Hungary they taught Sandor Vorody in History.

"The Wall" they called his chapter. Two years before the end of World War II. Sandor Vorody was a forty-year-old Marxist, a wealthy intellectual who placed great faith in the equality and justice communism could bring to his country. He turned his fortune over to the Hungarian resistance, financing what he called the printed revolution — underground journals, the only uncensored communication available to Hungarians during the war.

Then something happened that turned Grigor Vorody's father from a popular figure into a national legend.

In 1942, as the Nazis were weakened by the Russians, they frantically hunted down the opposition, bringing the resistance movement to a halt. All printing presses were found and confiscated, those who operated them tortured and killed. Many talked, and a chain reaction of unwilling betrayals followed. By early 1943 the resistance was almost shattered.

The five survivors of the resistance caucus gathered one morning in the basement of a sculptor's studio. Upstairs, they could hear a bust of Hitler being carved in Italian marble.

"It might take a long time before we can attack, months. Maybe even years," one of the five men said. "The Germans have enough power left in them to last, unless the allies come to our rescue."

Another man, bearded, tall, called by the code name Fire, punched the round wooden table. "The Americans will not come." The table cracked and everyone held their hard breath.

"Still, we must give people something to hope for, to keep fighting."

"We need presses, somewhere they can't be found."

"We need more than that." That was Fire again, his voice an octave lower than the others. "We need a man. One man who will be there day and night, working those presses. Alone, without contact.

"The comrade will print a daily message. We will circulate it by kids on bicycles and word of mouth, everywhere in Hungary. He will prepare the country for the revolution."

The five men spoke until dusk.

The plan was ready. What they needed now was a volunteer. That man would give them months, maybe years, of his life without contact with the outside. He would be built into a small space with his printing press, without door or window, or possibility to come out. Likely he would not come out at all, killed by a bomb or a fire that would fill his lungs with smoke long before his body burned. If he survived, he'd face the new world or a firing squad.

As the night fell upon Budapest and the sound of sirens warned of another air attack, they pulled the five straws that Sandor Vorody held the bottom halves well hidden in his palm. The shortest would be the one.

He wasn't sure his voice didn't precede him when he stopped the first fellow from drawing the straw that would mean his life.

"Let's stop this now, comrades. I'll be the one."

At first they protested, asking that fate be allowed to decide.

"But it is destiny," Vorody assured them. "It is my destiny. I'm the only one here who can operate a printing press. And I am writer. It's what I do, I write."

He put his wife and son on the last train to Paris on a pass that cost them their summer house.

Two comrades took him to the attic where he would work and live for as long as it took for the world to change. He watched them build the wall four feet away, brick by brick, until he could see just the top of their heads. The next day, from his attic, he sent his first message.

"I will be buried alive for Hungary, until you get together and tear down Nazism and my wall."

The printed pages came in batches of a hundred rolled out through a ragged slit a foot wide in the wall where bricks appeared shattered by a bomb. Food, water and air came through there too, and, over the 26 months he spent in his torture chamber, Nazi uniforms more than once blocked that narrow opening to the world. But they didn't find him. No one did. The plan worked.

At the end, there was the deafening noise of street fighting. "This is it then," he said out loud. Fire quickly heated the air, making it painful to inhale.

Later there was silence. Soldiers dying quietly, mothers bent over their wounded children. He couldn't know who had won.

For two days he lay on his cot, unmoving, taking shallow breaths to preserve the thin, precious air. No contact yet. Only two men knew where he was buried. Were they still alive?

The third day his mouth was too dry to swallow and his mind no longer functioned. Trapped in his coffin, hopeless, he couldn't tell if it was night or day. He thought he had been there longer. Weeks maybe. He was surprised he could still breathe. But he wondered how long he could live without water. Weeks? Days? He had read that somewhere, sometime. How little attention one paid to life. Its details. How precious they seemed to him now, how important.

Soon he would use his gun.

He could barely hear the sound of hammers when they came at last, only four feet away. They found him still alive, still breathing, but unconscious. His eyesight was permanently damaged, the capacity to distinguish color forever lost. From then on, his was a world in black and white. His body had reverted to the size of a child.

But no matter. They had won!

He asked for nothing in return. The country's greatest hero was simply grateful that communism and he were both alive.

Hungary's new leaders, his former comrades and a few overnight heroes he had never met, asked him to join the party executive. "You can pick your function — anything. Anything you want."

But he declined.

"I am not a politician. I want to be free to live in this new Hungary, with my wife and child. And to write."

He sent for Magda and Grigor and settled in their vast family compound overlooking the Danube, watching the great river flow merrily through the new world he had helped create.

Power was assigned swiftly under the new regime, and the prime minister personally asked Vorody to become communist Hungary's first ambassador to Washington. He refused a few times but in the end he was compelled to accept. The comrades were right. Hungary needed him again. He was wealthy by birth therefore American riches could not lure him. He was the only one among the country's new, working class leaders who spoke English fluently.

Magda and Grigor packed their bags again and crossed the Atlantic by boat, for the first time.

That's where it stopped. That's all she ever learned about Sandor Vorody. Kay closed the file again, and placed it back in its envelope.

She didn't hear much about the years following, his work in America or his return to Hungary where he eventually died. If the story was true, it was impressive. Her father had believed Sandor Vorody was genuine, but tragically mistaken. A real hero who sacrificed for the wrong cause.

She remembered her teacher, Madame Ilona, shedding tears when she read "The Wall" to them in first grade. She remembered the school plays in which she played various roles in "The Wall." The first boy who kissed her on the lips played Sandor Vorody. He was shorter than she was so she had to bend a little and slide her head forward, like a pelican. In grade two she played Comrade Fire, dressed in men's clothes because there weren't enough boys in her class. At every May Day anniversary, she was a member of the choir praising the Wall Hero. One year she was a flame, dancing around the wall behind which lay Sandor Vorody.

Still, what clues could there be in this story? What other mystery could the legend hold? What was there in the father's life that could lead her to his son?

She read again the printout of the E-mail and kept repeating it, like an incantation, long after she sealed the brown envelope and sent it to Stevie. Perhaps the answer really was in that envelope, and if it was, Stevie would help her find him at last.

"If you still want The Inquisitor, check the father, Sandor Vorody."

* * *

Odessa, USSR, 1985

September comes sharply in Odessa. What with the wind sweeping over the Black Sea bringing the smell of raw salt and Russian caviar all the way from sturgeon waters, making a brief halt to gain strength from the Danube River then blasting huge breakers along the Turkish, Bulgarian and Romanian shores, it has a way of letting you know that the season had changed. Any day now it would begin to rain.

The beach was empty that day, and so was the Soviet resort, except for the tall, middle-aged gentleman in his wet suit, the old fisherman in a broken boat careened by the last sand bank and a few Russian sailors on leave from the border post. They had walked the eight miles from their base to Odessa to catch the last few days of summer, and now they were camped on the beach making giant fires, drinking Stolichnaya, frying smelts and playing the balalaika in front of the deserted Coliseum Hotel. Others lay half naked in shabby jodhpurs and heavy boots, Kalishnikovs at their feet, scattering ashes, corks and fish bones, making out with the gypsy girls who passed at sunset peddling corn on the cob, fortunes and American Kents.

The tall gentleman advanced unnoticed by the soldiers into the cold water.

"It's going to rain tonight, tovarich Vorody." The wind amplified the raspy voice of the old fisherman. "The fish tell me there's going to be a storm. See those clouds? See how they gather in fours?"

The tall man lowered his visor and looked at the sky. All he could see was the sun, one last slice of red light falling into black water.

Ever since he became secret service chief, the Inquisitor rented the same dacha in Odessa, not far from the hotel where the tourists came, a place where he could always be seen. He went there alone, always in August and often overstayed the season. Sometimes he was there as late as mid-September, long after the crowds waned. Ivan Vassilich, the old fisherman, sometimes took him far into the water on his boat for some deep sea diving. Each summer day at sunset, even when a storm was announced for the night, the Inquisitor took his long solitary swim.

There was nothing unusual about this day.

"I like it when I have to fight the sea, Ivan Vassilich," he told the fisherman. "It fights better than most men."

That night Grigor swam well. He had to. Pushing hard against the waves in ink-colored water, ducking below the surface every time a flash of lightning lit up the sky like a reflector, he knew that Racklee could not wait much longer with the storm advancing as fast as it was towards the shore. But Grigor was not worried. He had practiced for this all his life.

He reached in three hours the spot beyond the Russian borders and into Turkish sea, where beautiful *Clara* waited. Racklee rented *Clara* from the Turkish government for a scientific underwater expedition. This time he played a marine explorer and head of ocean research at Yale University. The underwater capsule traveled without a hitch to shore.

In Istanbul the next morning, two middle-aged men, a redhead and a nondescript brunet, took a commercial flight to Aruba. From there, a cruise ship brought them to Miami.

SEVEN

"It's bad news, Bob. She's starting to rub Congress the wrong way."

The President stood silent, looking onto the gray courtyard off Leduc's quarters.

"How many days has it been?" he finally asked.

"Ten."

"She's doing well with the press. She nailed Koppel last night on "Nightline," after he sprung Florence Glaser on her."

"Sure did. Koppel called afterwards. He thinks she's the cat's ass."

"And Sally? The day-after interview with the two torture victims worked out great."

"That took care of the first days. But even Charlie Rose asked her about her past."

"I missed it."

Leduc touched the intercom and turned to the President. "Anything to drink?" Stone shook his head.

"More coffee for me, Joan. And the Rose report."

Less than three seconds later, the secretary brought in a stack of typed pages and a small cup of coffee.

She walked quickly to a green sofa and tucked in the white tail of a bed sheet.

"Anything else?" she asked.

Leduc turned back to Stone, flipping the pages.

"Here it is. Her answer to Rose. 'The only troubling thing about me, Charlie, is that I don't underestimate the public, like the media do. The media thrive on gossip and I thrive on issues. That's what troubles me. Americans want to know what I stand for.'" He looked at Stone, a question mark in his eyes.

"Go on. I like it so far. Go on."

He paced the room slowly, trying to stay within the range of a slim draft coming from the open window. The shirt he put on just an hour before stuck to his back like a wet rag.

Leduc's voice went to a dull baritone when he read Rose's part.

"How do you respond to the accusations about your private life?"

"That my private life is my own. And my public life belongs to everyone in our country, to everyone whose human rights are in jeopardy.'"

Stone loosened his tie.

"We needed a straight arrow, remember?" he noted, his throat scratchy from the heat.

"I thought so, Bob, just like you did. Now I'm not so sure."

"The print media?"

"She had a cover story in *People*. Turned out good. Hiked up the polls a bit. And she placed a few good angles with *Time*. Great photo spreads. But she's too beautiful, see what I mean? Even that doesn't work like we thought. People are afraid of her. Women resent her. Men want her. And what makes it worse is she's not married."

"How about Congress?"

"The problem is she sticks to her guns. She doesn't compromise."

The President sat on the small sofa, trying it for comfort.

"Do you sleep here a lot?" he asked, absently.

"Now and then. Why?"

"No, nothing. Just — the heat."

Leduc's bony shoulders shrugged and the small head bent forward, preoccupied.

"Any IOU's being called in?" the President asked.

"Plenty. Everyone wants his own man in for human rights. You name it. Blacks, natives, gays, feminists, preachers, mothers, fetuses, transsexuals, students, teachers, sex offenders, death row inmates, —"

But Stone cut him short, laughing.

"At least on this one we don't have to deal with animal rights."

He rose abruptly and started pacing again. One more minute in this room and he was sure he'd develop a violent rash.

"Bob, the fact is we've got to get her to come up with something big."

"What kind of big?"

"Something so big it'll get their mind off this bullshit." Stone nodded, inching closer to the door.

Leduc pulled him back with the edge in his voice.

"Either she fixes it now, or she's out of the race."

Just then the phone rang. Leduc picked it up right away and his face loosened into a wide smile.

"Yes, Millicent. He's with me. All right then. I'll tell him. Can you hold on?"

He turned to the President, covering the mouthpiece with his fingers.

"Your wife is ready now, Bob. If you'd like to go, I can meet you —"

"No, it's all right Clancy, go on, I'll let you talk to her. I think I've got the idea. I'll meet with Kemeny and Endicott tomorrow."

The cool air of the antechamber flowed at last through the open door. The President rushed out.

* * *

Stevie Vitt opened the door just a crack, leaving the heavy chain in place and peered through the one way viewer.

"Friends on the horizon," Kay said, winking at the invisible eye on the other side.

The door burst wide open and Stevie came out to greet her.

"Oh God, I can't believe it." Kay held him by his strong, muscular arms. "I can't believe how dashing you look. I forget after I don't see you for a while and then boom, you shock me."

"But you said that I wasn't your type."

"I lied."

"It's so good to see you, Kay. You look great. I'm so happy to see you get what you want."

He hugged her again.

"Come on. Come inside."

Stevie's apartment was small and functional, unadorned. Square leather sofa, the color of Italian mud. A bent crystal sheath for a coffee table. A small African rug. Neither he nor Tommy had any time for household duties — the only place Stevie had filled with gadgets was the kitchen. He loved to cook.

"Where's Tom Cruise?" Kay asked opening the narrow cupboard where she knew there would be a water glass.

"I'm glad he's not around to hear this. He told me he'll spank you if you call him that again."

He pulled Kay's glass from her hands just before she took it to her lips.

"Wait. Don't drink that. It's polluted, or didn't you hear. That stuff is full of lead, and we're all a big science experiment." He handed her a chilled bottle of Evian.

"Oh yes," she sighed with delight, gulping down the water to the last drop. "I needed this. It's so hot out there.

"So tell me. Where is he?"

"I sent him out. I'm not sure he should know in detail what you and I are talking about."

Kay watched Stevie fix himself a vodka martini.

"What's cooking?" she asked, following him around the counter to the sofa. The leather made a squishy sound when they sat. It felt cool but sticky under her. She hated leather for clothes or furniture. But men liked it — Tony, Tommy, Stevie. Even the man she couldn't help thinking about.

"Stuffed oysters to start. Then salmon."

"I don't mean dinner. Though I'm famished. I mean what's cooking work-wise. What's doing at DEA?"

"Not good, as I'm sure you've heard. Not for me, anyway. I'm stuck in Siberia compiling statistics on Mexican Quaalude manufacturers while the kids in the street 'chase dragons' and I can't catch the bastards who supply them. It's frustrating as hell. But right now, there's no way out. Not since I crossed CIA on that passenger plane bombing."

"I know. I haven't seen you since then. I'm so sorry."

"It's almost a year now and I still can't get used to the idea that you can lose your career just for doing your job."

"What happened to the guy who got you in this mess?'

"Jacobi? It wasn't really his fault, you know. He and I shared information, we each worked on our case. I guess you never heard the whole story. Basically, DEA had me tracking a Syrian drug lord who had a shipment on that plane and Jacobi was working for the airline chasing down the terrorists who checked the bomb in the same piece of luggage."

"I heard he actually screwed you somehow. At least that's what Ed told me."

Stevie looked around the room nervously. His voice suddenly lowered.

"He didn't screw me. He used what I gave him in his client's court case. It was his job, as an investigator."

"But how come you gave him DEA information?"

"Because my superiors checked him out and okayed it. Hell, they pushed me to it. They said go for it, that little Mossad mole is a gold mine of information. See what goodies you can trade."

"So they turned on you after the story went public?" asked Kay.

"Yes. CIA went ballistic and my superiors suddenly lost their memory. I was left to take the fall."

"So Jacobi got you in trouble anyway."

"He got himself in trouble too. He dug out the truth. He was smart. Put everything together and got to the ugliest mess I've ever come across in my life."

Stevie got up abruptly and closed the blinds. He turned on the radio, loud, fixed himself another drink and came back near Kay. He spoke close to her ear.

"CIA sent Justice after me, forced me to sign an affidavit denouncing Jacobi as a liar. They smeared him in the press and in court. They billed him as an opportunist, a fraud."

"I know. I've read that."

He inched even closer, his breath hot and harsh, tingling Kay's ear drum.

"And they've done worse. You don't want to know how much worse."

Kay shuddered. She never thought she'd have to sit through whispered conversations and radio clutter again. This felt a lot like another world. Another time.

"How the hell were you supposed to know the CIA was indirectly involved in the bombing of that plane?"

"No, the question is, how can they live with themselves after 259 people died because they protected that drug shipment?"

He moved back to the other end of the sofa, his chiseled body tense, his high forehead drenched in sweat despite the coolness of the room. He pushed his thick blond hair off his face and looked at her, his eyes cloudy with an anger Kay had never seen before.

"Anyway," he spoke again, after a moment. "Back to your question. Jacobi is around. In fact I had him in mind for you. Vorody's trail starts in Europe. Jacobi has access to the right network in Frankfurt, Paris, London — he's been working it for twenty years. Going there without him would be a waste of time. I'll ask him and he'll do it. He owes me."

Kay watched Stevie set the simple, glass coffee table with two black vinyl squares and white plates. His strong hands seemed awkward handling the small silverware and the fragile wine glass. She rose to help, but he pushed her back on the sofa, gently.

"Drug dealers and dinner are my specialty."

She had met Stevie Vitt at the same time she met Ed Endicott. Ed had been a passerby in a Central Park drug shooting. Stevie was the DEA agent tailing a major drug lord who walked into an ambush. And Kay the prosecutor of the surviving assassin. She smiled remembering how impressive they both were. Stevie with his green eyes deep like twin lakes, and his confidence, poise and track record. He was a rising star at DEA. And Ed with his patrician features and Saville Row tweeds, the eminent lawyer. A prosecutor's dream witness.

She saved Ed then. She had sensed he was gay from the start. And this was Central Park, at 82nd Street, well past midnight. She didn't have much doubt what had brought the prominent lawyer there so she arranged with the defense lawyer to skip that line of questioning. She risked very little since her case was solid, and she gained a great friend. Two great friends, because in the process she also got to know Stevie. Ed went on to become a senator, and her Washington ally.

"What did you find out about the E-mail?" she asked Stevie after dinner. The radio was still on, but now it was playing Chopin, softly.

"I asked Tommy to trace it at FBI. Apparently they can't. There's a way to send these things without leaving any signals."

"Who could it be?"

"Most likely a prank. Or maybe just a false lead, something to send you on a wild goose chase. Anybody who wanted to really help you would have given you more."

Kay made a conscious effort to dismiss a wave of impatience. Why was it that both Stevie and Ed took that message so lightly?

"You read the father's file I sent you?"

"Yes. I studied it. It's pretty clear — the legend part. I made all the inquiries I could from this end without taking any chances. He was Hungary's ambassador in Washington and Grigor went to school here. I can't go any further without tipping somebody off. It's time to go to Europe. But first I have to reach Jacobi."

"Did old man Vorody come back here after they went back to Hungary?"

"No. Neither father nor son. The father died soon after they returned, when Grigor was twenty-six, first year in KGB academy."

"Is there anything at all in the father's history to point out what Grigor is doing now? Or what happened to him after he left Russia in 1985? Or why he did leave? Any motivations?"

"Nothing, from what I can see."

Kay got up to leave. It was past 11 pm and she still had a lot of work ahead of her, if she was going to prepare properly for the first bluff of her political career. Her voice quivered when she spoke.

"The thing is, Stevie, if I don't get something solid on Vorody fast, they'll withdraw my nomination. There is a lot of backlash against me."

"How solid does it have to be? And when do you have to have it?"

"Yesterday…I need a photograph. A passport. A changed name. An address, ideally. If you have to travel, do it immediately."

* * *

"Ed?"

"Yes." It was midnight and Ed liked to fall asleep early.

"I went to see Stevie."

"And?"

"He asked around, checked out the file, and he thinks he can help me."

"Kay, are you sure you want to do this? I mean we could run into big trouble if we produce nothing."

"This is the only way to get the two things that matter to me, Ed. I want to be confirmed. And I want Vorody."

* * *

The President called a meeting the next day.

The Oval Office seemed smaller now, less imposing. Behind the dark mahogany desk, still finishing a telephone conversation, was a man who made Kay feel instantly at home. Ed Endicott accompanied her, at the President's request.

"Settle in, this will be a long one, missed seeing you Kay." Stone waved them in, still holding the receiver, and gestured the steward to bring in a tray of lemonade. He went on with his call in muted voice, almost a whisper, gentle and caring to the person at the other end. Undoubtedly something personal, Kay thought, fighting the urge to listen.

"Long one?" muttered Endicott. "I wonder what he has in mind."

"I think I know what it is," she spoke calmly, detached. "I think he's getting tired of the pressure. Why should he fight for me?"

She was surprised at how easy it was to acknowledge her fear.

"Don't be absurd. He loves you."

But did he, she wondered. Did he?

Stone turned halfway toward them again and pulled a long, silver fountain pen from its marble pedestal. He started scribbling quickly, stopping now and then for a sip of lemonade, listening intently to the person on the other end. Nobody listened like him. Nobody was as good at making people feel that they mattered.

They had been there for only five minutes and already it seemed like hours. Lately, time had extended for Kay in ways she never knew possible. It stretched, long, eternal. Days became weeks, the change brought about by a simple minute more germane to her destiny than years of her past life. The twelve days she had survived as candidate felt longer than her entire life. Now every moment counted. In a mere instant there was everything to lose. Everything to gain.

"These have been the longest days of your life haven't they Kay?" Stone asked, hanging up.

Before she could tell him he'd read her mind again, he continued.

"I bet Ed thinks we're doing well with this nomination. So far so good, right, Senator?"

"Indeed we are," said Endicott.

"Kay is good on camera, isn't she?"

"Splendid. I don't know if you watched it, but she killed them on "Nightline." And on 'Charlie Rose.'"

"I was also impressed with the interview in *People*."

"Well, Bob, if you must know, the editor is a dear friend."

An awkward silence followed. The senator continued.

"And she photographs very well."

Stone stared blankly well above Endicott's shoulder.

"Photographs cannot do justice to someone as beautiful as Kay."

Kay's breath quickened in expectation, in fear of what he might say.

"Senator, I once told you. I cannot afford to fuck up a nomination again."

None of them had heard him utter such words before. They were stunned.

"You're a genuine bastard, you know that?" Kay said after catching her breath.

The air in the room stood still. There was no breeze from the open window, as if the moment was frozen in a video frame.

The silence broke spectacularly when the presidential line rang. Stone, composed, whispered a postponement and hung up, his eyes fixed on her.

She spoke on cue, brisk and clear, stating rather than sharing what she had to say.

"I guess I better get used to it. If I stick around, I'll see this side of you again."

"If I let you stick around," Stone said calmly and rose, as if to say good-bye.

Kay edged near him, sharply. They were closer than they had ever been, except the night he held her, that last night.

"Because you will ask me to withdraw, won't you? Because you will give in to pressure groups. You've done it before."

"Before what?"

"Before you figured out you needed someone like me to come to your rescue, to show everyone that you care about something other than winning another four years."

She was scared, yes, but she knew she could not stop now.

"Well, use me now that you've got me. Use what I stand for and what I'm worth and what I represent. What are you afraid of, Stone? Are you afraid to stand by me?

"Look, I know I must do something. I'm working on it. I'm timing myself to release information that will change the balance of things. I know how to play, I know how to gamble, but I need to take my own risks."

Stone rested against his tall chair, impenetrable. On his face, a brief smile traveled fleetingly.

"You're quite extraordinary."

Kay's eyes opened wide, unable to guess what he would decide. Her fate clung to the breath he took before changing the course of her life.

"I'll let you stay in the race."

Her body relaxed.

"But something big must happen, and you must make it happen immediately."

Then, abrupt and suddenly weary, speaking as if Endicott was absent, he focused solely on Kay.

"Do you still want him or should I give you another man? You'll need all the help you can get."

"How many days can you give me before you ask for my withdrawal again?"

"You're not withdrawn. It was now or never. From now on, it's in your hands. All bets are off."

Kay sighed, relieved. She looked him in the eye and answered firmly.

"I'll stay with Ed."

* * *

Even as he grew more optimistic about the Vorody solution, Ed couldn't help feeling frightened by the mystery surrounding the case.

Kay had gathered enough information to prosecute The Inquisitor on the two murder cases — one in New York and one in Miami — provided he could be arrested on American soil. But all those years Kay had tried to get an accurate record of Vorody in FBI or CIA files, and there was nothing. Not a photograph, not a fingerprint, not a single piece of information. Every road was blocked, every file sealed or lost, every key to the puzzle missing or worse, leading to another labyrinth with no exit. Vorody was everywhere and nowhere, as if he had a hundred lives. The head of the Hungarian secret service and Pavlov's right hand, the most dangerous and the most wanted man in the Eastern Bloc had vanished somewhere in America.

* * *

"I like the other shirt better for that suit, honey. The one on top, the dove-gray." Eva said, coming from the downstairs kitchen.

Ezra Jacobi pulled a new shirt from the neat stack and began to unfold it, careful not to hit a pin.

From his window, he could see the sky over Manhattan. It was like that shirt — gray. And prickly. He could swear there was a dove nesting on the balcony.

"The car is here, Jacobi!" Eva's voice came to him, raw, like crystals about to break. Impatient.

They had met in high school in Tel Aviv, and even now, more than twenty-five years later, she still called him by his last name. At least his kids still called him Daddy. Give them time, little *mechablims*, give them time.

Jacobi glanced quickly at his watch. His flight was in an hour and JFK was an hour away. Good enough. Who likes to wait in an airport lounge? He looked at himself one more time in the full length mirror. He pulled in his belly and buttoned his jacket high, then unbuttoned it all the way. One of these days he'd have to get new clothes.

"Coming, Eva!"

He hurried down the stairs.

Just then his cellular phone rang.

"Hello!" he said, his small suitcase already in one hand and his passport heavy in his breast pocket.

"Jacobi. Hi, long time no hear. It's me — Stevie."

EIGHT

It was at times like this he thought he might let go.

The Inquisitor took the wooden doll from the empty shelf of a room previous inhabitants had called the study. The doll was red, green and yellow, with hips, breasts and hairline painted in a rough black crayon. The wide-set eyes were carved and colorless, like two forgotten holes through which you could see blond wood in awkward contrast to the rest of the glazed surface. He was a grown man when he picked it up at a country fair in Leningrad. He was following a Russian whose daughter was leaking information to the British. She had been arrested and executed earlier that day but her father didn't know, and he was buying a gift for her birthday. The imperfect doll fell from the brown wrapping when they took him, and the man who ordered his daughter's killing felt strangely compelled to give it a home.

The television set in the room he used for sleeping buzzed for a while because of the impending storm. When it cleared, he could hear, again, Kemeny's announcement. "I will say only that we have major new leads. We are very close to capturing and prosecuting Grigor Vorody."

He started to rotate the doll's head, carefully. Half of the body came unhinged and from within another head, smaller, less flawed, rose toward him. Then another. And another. The last doll was small as a finger tip and painted just as intricately as the others. When it came off, its shiny head, much better preserved than the matrix, released a whiff of dust. The Inquisitor pulled from the doll's belly a coil of celluloid tightly wound and secured with a minuscule string. A vague perfume emanated from the hidden space, unlocking a tide of memories.

The last time he saw Father.

He is frail. It is hard for him to take the last trip to the Farm. He looks older, much older than just a few months ago when they spent Christmas at the Embassy. His eyes seem empty. His voice shallow. Life streams out of him quickly.

"This is it son, we're going back to Hungary."

Grigor is twenty-five.

"For how long?" he asks.

"You'll know that when the time comes, from Racklee."

"Why now?"

"It's time, son. I have to bring you in myself. And it's getting late for me."

They leave for Budapest that night, to a home he saw sometimes in his dreams. It is large, gothic and drafty, a fortress more than a house, a place where he is never warm, where clothes don't dry for days and where the sheets, always wet, cling to his body. A giant shadow edging on a rock promontory above the Danube. From his window he can see the gray sky pour over the entire city.

Father kept dying for almost a year. Next went Mother, who broke a hip coming home from his forty-day wake and refused surgery. They buried her in a different tomb, in another area of the same cemetery. She could not share the glory of her husband in the lot reserved for national heroes. He tried then for the first time to reconstruct what happened to Sandor Vorody. He stumbled, and failed, mostly. Mired in Father's absence, he tried desperately to remember his words, always elusive and scarce, the words he so avariciously kept to himself all his life. But he discovered that, far from illuminating the large patches of darkness which tormented him, Sandor's words narrowed even more the already tight corridor to the truth. Often he wondered if it wasn't just that he himself was guilty of a selective memory. Selecting what he could live with was the only way he knew how to deal with the colossal task of rewriting Sandor Vorody and Hungary's history.

Later he tried again. He talked for hours on end with Racklee. He looked for clues to the giant riddle that brought him where he was, but again truth escaped through his fingers. He kept his mind intact, knowing that death awaited him at the end of each road if he failed — and if he succeeded. He worked. He didn't think much about who he was. He did the job for everyone. He prided himself on the tasks at hand. Like the Disinformation Ministry. Still, there were nights where he woke up at dawn, bathed in sweat, searching for his real self, only to see it from a distance, growing smaller each time, like a piece of ice melting in the heat of his complicated destiny.

Was it Father's fault or was it just that history itself had been so consistently misleading? He kept searching for an answer. He pieced every thread, tied every knot and wove in every shadow. At last, he had a picture — pale, faded, and ever changing. A picture of who his father had been, a picture of his own unsettling, unacceptable reality. But even as he drew that picture he knew that it was nothing more than a projection of the past. The story of a story. A draft, a distant draft which, even as he thought back on it now, amid broken dolls in the room others called Study, kept changing, ever changing in his mind.

The Inquisitor pulled the pale string that held together the fragile piece of celluloid. The film uncoiled obediently under his fingers. Through his skin, through his veins, through his membranes, traveled the uncertain outline of his father's story.

The time was the 1950's. Soon after he came to America as Hungarian ambassador, Sandor Vorody learned that, at the other end of the world, on the banks of the Danube, the Hungary he had dreamed of was far from happening.

The fight for power had brought out the worst in his fellow resistance fighters, many of whom were now jailed and executed at the hand of their own comrades, with mock trials or without any trial at all. A new class had formed very quickly, one that stole the wealth of the capitalists, killed them, raped their children, and took over their role. The poor simply replaced the rich, trading one class for another. Only the new ruling class was far worse. Uneducated, illiterate, they had come to power through violence and betrayal. Once in power, they didn't know how to manage it, and thrived only on consumption, creating nothing in return. Ruin was imminent for anyone who had eyes to see.

Stories came filtering into their rich Georgetown house, stories of abuse and anarchy. Of violence. Of personal and political gain. Father's Jewish friends were once again persecuted, this time because their role in the resistance entitled them to positions in the new regime. Sources brought to Sandor Vorody cases of assassination, of political imprisonment without trial for critics of the regime. Word was coming every day of another freedom fighter tortured and killed in Stalin's prison camps. The death toll had risen well above Hitler's. Fascism was reinterpreted and applied to a new set of beliefs. Only this time the power structure was much stronger.

As if that were not enough to sadden Father, Hungary was also fraught with poverty and hunger, in proportions that never existed before.

How could they have been so blind? Not just him and his comrades, but their idols, Marx, Engels, Lenin?

Witnessing the unraveling of history as him had made it, Sandor Vorody knew he had created a monster.

He grew obsessed with the damage he had done.

"Listen to these youngsters Magda, listen to them," Grigor heard him tell his wife more than once. "This is not about Hungary anymore. If they win, there will be no place to go. No place at all. Our son will have no future in this world we created."

But Father was the Wall hero. He was a fighter. A tired fighter, drained physically and spiritually by the catastrophic results of his war, but a fearless fighter nonetheless. I made it, I can kill it, he thought sadly, as he walked over to his first meeting with the CIA.

It was easy to contact Donovan without raising suspicion. Vorody was a hugely trusted man, Hungary would never dream of him playing against them. And the founding father of OSS believed him.

But what was hard was what Donovan had in mind for him. He couldn't do anything relevant himself, they told him. He was trusted by the new rulers of Hungary, yes, but he was also kept away from the action. They would never harm him because he was their greatest hero, which is why they were afraid of him. This regime was here to stay for a long time. The fight would take decades, maybe more. America was prepared for a hundred years' war — was he? The game had two names: patience and sacrifice.

So they asked Father to sacrifice what he loved most.

That's all he knew. Pieced from his mother's secret accounts, Racklee's measured allowances, "I know nothing more. They would not tell me," and the dying Sandor Vorody's fragmented memories.

Though by that time, besieged by the present, his father's world had entirely dissolved in the past. The Wall was all he wanted to think about. His survival behind it, fueled by hope, had taken over completely and he became convinced that it was then and there he had lived his happiest days. The magical past which when he lived it had seemed so unbearable, had now won the battle over the rest of his life. Even his black and white eyesight had become a treasured gift. "I now dream the blue of the sky." he'd say. "And it's always perfect. If I could see its true blue each day I know I'd be disappointed. I've selected the best memory."

Grigor discarded the halved dolls directly into the ocean.

The wooden pieces glistened, floating on the crest of a small wave. When he died, he would not have his father's consolation. He was not a hero. He had sacrificed too many.

A pearl pink shell, locked and wobbly, washed against his foot and cracked open. He picked it up and his hands lingered for a moment on the translucent surface. The rosy flesh pulsated desperately between his fingers. He watched in silence the primordial struggle. He shut the shell tight, and felt life quiver within. He placed it carefully in the warm sand below the water, and watched it sail away.

How could he think he would tire of it?

Tonight of all nights, life seemed so alluring and so undeniable. Life, even his life, was worth fighting for.

He looked far into the naked night, searching for the enemy. He was hunted. In his pocket, wound with its fragile string, was his weapon.

NINE

Frankfurt, Germany

Ezra Jacobi met Stevie Vitt for breakfast at the Frankfurter Hof Hotel. He came down late and found Stevie immersed in his *Herald Tribune* at a table facing the entrance to the crowded dining room.

"Bad habit, Stevie boy," he said right in his friend's ear, startling him. "Never forget to check the room with the corner of your eyes even when you're reading the basketball score."

Stevie laughed and shook his hand.

"Hey, how are you? Want something to eat?"

"You're kidding me?' the Israeli said, his eyes sunny like two Mediterranean olives. His tanned bald head and round face sparkled under the glossy dining room lights. "I'm starving." He led the way to the lavish buffet and Stevie followed.

"Good to see you," Jacobi said, piling eggs and German sausage on his plate near a mound of something yellow and oily.

"If Eva finds out you're eating pork..." Stevie teased. He hadn't seen Jacobi for more than a year but everything about him made it seem like yesterday.

"So who's gonna tell her?" Jacobi snapped back.

"What's the gooey stuff?" Stevie asked, spooning onto his plate a healthy serving of fruit, bran flakes and yogurt.

"Cod fish mashed with oil and garlic. The Germans make this better than the French, believe me."

Back to the table, Stevie observed, "Lots of Arabs here this morning. What do you make of it?"

"A terrorist convention." Jacobi replied, looking around the room gleefully, but stopped when he saw the unsettled look on Stevie's face. "Hey, don't worry, I didn't ask you to fly here for nothing. I'll take the time to look for your man."

"We need the information fast."

"I've already made some calls and we have an appointment with men who can help, in Wiesbaden."

"What have you heard so far?"

"Just that your man is bad news."

"By the way, she got a second message."

"So?" Jacobi looked up from his plate. "What did it say?"

"To look for a connection between our man and someone called Racklee."

Jacobi got up, abruptly.

"You want anymore?"

"No, thanks. I'm not even half done".

"Come on. Get up and keep me company.'

They weren't even near the buffet when the Israeli started talking, firing his words rapidly.

"That's what my sources said. But don't use that name. Not at the table. Not anywhere."

"Who is he? I've seen that name somewhere before."

"I'm sure you have. He's the leader of the Cowboys. Agents gone bad. Former CIA's who were involved in the Iran Contra affair. Big mercenary — arms, drugs, you name it. Except he doesn't do it for the money. He does it for the 'American Century.' I haven't come up against him myself personally, but it's a fact that his group was involved in our airline case. He's the momzer who got Justice on my case. And they say I was lucky. I hear he's the worst kind of enemy."

Suddenly, Stevie remembered where he had seen the name. Reference was made to it in four separate cases of drugs for arms deals. Every time the DEA was ready to make a bust somebody tipped the target. And that name was the link between those cases.

"Did he arrange for this wild goose chase? Empty files everywhere, no record of U.S. entry? Does he have that kind of reach? And why would he bother?"

"This is The Question, Stevie. We have to ask it very quietly, in the right places," he said, looking serious and putting his index finger to his lips. "Very, very quietly."

Jacobi loaded another plate, this time with sweets, and grabbed a small bowl of dates he handed to Stevie.

"Here. Carry this for me."

They sat for awhile, munching quietly.

"So who are you working for this time, Mr. Terrorist Hunter?"

Jacobi shrugged. "Good question."

"Plenty of what you're after's in this room, am I right?"

"Plenty."

He scanned the room and his eyes stopped on the left corner.

"Check out the two Arabs there. See them? Definitely *mechablims*. Terrorists. Planning the next hit." Stevie nodded. "Don't worry. Nothing will happen here." Jacobi's eyes moved like radar onto the next table. "And the Russian there, sitting with a guy with ears like an elephant. Elephant ears is Baader Meinhoff, minor league six years ago but now looks like he's got better company." He wiped his chin with the red damask napkin and took a sip of his coffee.

"Nah. I'm not chasing any of them."

He pointed with his eyes to a spot to Stevie's left.

"But those two are. The two kids wearing the same blouson."

Stevie could see them without turning.

"They're Mossad. Just flew in. Too much in a hurry to wear the shirts they bought on sale outside. In my days they'd send some old German survivor who'd blend in with his bagel and tea and an old magazine. Now they've got shoppers. They put the old folk out to pasture." Jacobi laughed.

"What's so funny?"

"I'm just laughing because I would not work nowadays for Mossad. I told them — when they were accusing me of spying for the Israelis. I told the CIA I'll work for anyone who pays the bills. And that's not Mossad, believe me."

A sudden weariness crept onto Jacobi's face. Stevie turned and followed his eyes.

"What's the matter?"

"The two Syrians who walked in. There. By the entrance."

"With the shoulder bags?"

"Yeah, in the green windbreakers."

"So?"

"They're advance men. Shooters. They're checking the place out to make sure it's safe for the financiers."

"What financiers?"

"The ones who pay for all this *shpookerai*."

"How do you know about them?"

"I don't," Jacobi said, tapping his finger to his temples. "But it's in here, Stevie boy. Human intelligence. Look around you. What more do you want?"

He reached into the bowl of dates and ate them slowly, sucking the pits. "Hmm," he purred. "This feels like home."

"How come I don't see any Americans?"

"Are you kidding me?" Jacobi laughed. "Your compatriots still don't believe terrorist groups get together. This room can't be seen from a spy satellite so it doesn't exist. It's Okay. One day the Brits will tell them."

Stevie smiled.

"You really underestimate us, Jacobi."

"Yeah?"

"We're not as stupid as you think." Stevie took a date from the bowl.

"Okay, fine, you've got a few good undercover agents. You've got some good cops too, like you. And what the hell good did it do you?"

Stevie's eyes clouded over and his voice grew husky.

"I meant to ask you. Would you have taken a classified file from me when we worked on the airline case?"

"Sure. I always trusted you."

Stevie tensed and looked away. His voice came out with difficulty.

"It's what they wanted —"

Jacobi's face was blank when he completed his sentence. "And you refused."
He looked down into his plate, filled with date pits, and sighed.
"Hey... I licked my wounds for awhile after they tried to indict me. But I'm back in business."
"I wish I could say the same thing."
"You will. You will this time." He gestured at the waiter scribbling the word 'Zall' in the air. "Just as soon as we find Vorody."

* * *

Kay returned to her suite at a little past ten. She felt exhausted, as if a part of her mind had been torn out, rolled into a ball and kicked around on a soccer field. Messages piled up on the Empire desk. She returned a few calls but the pile seemed to grow.
Tony, of course, left a few "urgent" reminders.

"Who died?" she asked, when she finally got him on the phone.
"You're lucky I don't hang up," he replied angrily.
"I saw all kinds of garbage in the press again. Get out of there and come home, Kay."
She was too tired to argue.
"I can't. I saw Stone today, and he's committed. It's too late to change anything now."
"But you're a ping pong ball for those assholes! They think they can do anything they want. It tells you about this country — these fucking leaders."
Kay was dead silent. Her veins pulsed so hard against her temples she wondered for a moment if they'd pop and kill her. The thought gave her relief. Let it be quick.
"Kay, doesn't it?"
She remained silent a moment too long and then blurted out:
"Sweetheart, grow up. All you really know how to do is pout."
Tony hung up.
She flicked the switch to the computer screen near the telephone looking for her E-mail. There were fifty messages waiting. Forget it. She clicked it off. She was curious to see if there was anything about Vorody from her unknown friends, but even Vorody could wait until tomorrow.

She took an aromatic bath, poured herself a glass of cool chardonnay and bit on one of the giant strawberries the hotel manager sent up every night. He remembered she once said she could live on chardonnay and strawberries.

Out on the terrace that circled her suite, she curled in one of the two white wicker chaises. Two chairs for one. She had never really known how to be part of a couple.

The night was perfect, stars bright and so close she wanted to reach out and pick one for herself. For luck. And the moon, pregnant and poetic, beamed a bouquet of fireworks, illuminating the city.

It was useless trying to empty her mind of him. The President. Kay found herself replaying images of him, his words, the sound of his voice. She smiled as she recalled her fiery monologue, his startled face, his hair, longish, tipped with silver. The way it brushed the nape of his neck, trapped at the edge of his collar.

She could hear his voice — disturbing. That voice when he was close to her. The intensity with which he looked at her when she spoke. His hands — fingers long and tapered, expressive, yet so masculine. Perfect. Esthetically perfect. And that faint fragrance of roses that followed him around, like an aura, coming from the White House gardens, as if the man and his surroundings had become one. A man in charge, who belonged everywhere he went, who felt at ease with the power he held over his country and over her life.

Kay thought she heard the door but ignored it, hoping she could take him with her to her dreams.

It was from the fragrance she knew he was there, standing beside her in the doorway, dressed in the same dark suit he wore that afternoon, the same collar, this time opened a bit, and his hands, those same hands, wrapped around a small bouquet of blush roses.

"I told the manager I'd deliver these myself."

She held her hand out for the flowers and, victim of the moment, they fell from his outstretched fingers. Petals spread like pink snow at Kay's feet.

"I'm sorry," she said and knelt down to gather them.

"Don't be." Because of a bunch of ruined roses, he reached for her.

He caught her as she rose to meet him, and when they touched, the electrical charge they had both tried so hard to tame finally ignited.

Everything felt right from then on. The way their lips touched, his mouth grazing hers, tormenting her and later biting hers deeply, urgently, her tongue soft and eager, surprising him at every turn, driving him mad with the need of her.

"I wanted you ever since I can remember," he said, and looked at her hard, hard enough to make her remove her robe slowly, hypnotized by his force.

"I wanted you even more."

They fit as if carved from the same mold. They moved in the same rhythm, their whispers asked and answered in perfect harmony, the flow of need and satisfaction so exquisite that it made them tremble at the thought of losing it.

They made love on the terrace under sparks of moon and falling stars. Afterwards, they lay close, her head fitting perfectly on his left shoulder, his arm curled around her waist and his left hand resting on her burning skin.

Stone had never been a tender lover, nor a considerate one. Even now he had made love to this woman fast and fiercely, but so very differently, clinging to her as if he feared something would take her away.

They rested, Kay falling into a light sleep while he, wide awake, explored her body. She was so beautiful and yet it was her flaws that touched him. The beauty mark on her left breast. The velvety skin between her legs, a touch soft and indulgent, just at the birth of her sex. Her lips, a bit too round, like a heart, quivering gently as she slept, the scar on her cheekbone still flushed by her body heat, her long and slender limbs curled instinctively around his left leg. This woman could love. She could think, run a country if she had to. And love. He caught himself wishing that he was someone else — anyone but Robert Stone.

He wanted her as she lay warm and sleeping, without will. He played with her, his perfect toy, enjoying the taste of her, making her moan and twist around him begging for more. She woke to sex with a man she could barely distinguish, large and dominant, riding above her, making her weak with desire. She followed his rhythm and obeyed his whispered instructions as he led her to a place where nothing, absolutely nothing was more important than his heartbeat against hers, the pulse of their bodies, his hands, and their immediate and insatiable need.

* * *

The next day, two people knew the President was a changed man. His favorite secret service guard, no-last-name-Roger, who had escorted Kay to the hotel and whose nature sealed his lips tighter than anyone's orders. And Kimberly Devane, who insisted she had to see him.

Stone went for his usual morning run. He had slept just two hours, then read the first media reaction to Kay's press announcement. She sure operated fast! She must have been ready for it all along. Good for her. It was a great stunt, assuming it worked. Assuming she had some real leads and some way to get to this Vorody guy before her time ran out. One thing was certain: no matter what he did this morning, he couldn't take his mind off Kay.

As always, Devane jogged along at his side. This morning Leduc had joined them, wheezing like an old radiator. The man had even stalked him at breakfast, with his hard line against "running after some Hungarian freak who's probably been dead and buried in Uzbekistan."

He made absolutely no sense. Stone could see no danger. Even if it didn't work in the end, it would occupy the media long enough to throw some water on that crazy coalition of Right to Lifers and radical feminists. Now how on earth did she manage to antagonize all of them?

"You're over-reacting, Clancy. Vorody has been sighted around Miami and New York. Furthermore, he's a suspect in two murders. That's enough for Justice to claim federal criminal jurisdiction. If she gets him it's a clear road to glory. And if she doesn't, it can't hurt to string the press along until she's confirmed."

His campaign manager looked pitiful this morning as he struggled to keep up.

"It's not going to be that simple. Suppose she doesn't get a thing on him? What if she's lying and gets caught? Worse, if God forbid CIA's involved?"

Stone exploded into laughter.

"You're completely paranoid, Leduc, you know that? Why does everything have to do with the CIA?"

"Put KGB in the sentence and it does, Bob," said Devane. "If they throw up national security objections at the trial, we'll have a firefight."

"Anyway," continued Leduc, irritated by the intervention of the VP he had nicknamed Baby Face. "We're letting her open a can of worms, Bob, and the can might explode in your face."

Devane was still working with Stone on the day's agenda when Kimberly called on his private line. He pretended it was Millicent.

"Hi honey. No, I'm not free at all today. Well, I'm sorry, I really am, I know it's important but I can't. Nope. Just no way."

The second time Kimberly called, Millicent was with him, working on a proposal to revamp the education system. Caught off guard, he agreed to meet her at 3 pm.

"Who was that?" asked his wife.

"Mother." He replied. "She's in town and wanted to come by."

They worked nonstop for the next hour. Millicent chaired the education task force and she was making great progress. Education was her background. She had earned nationwide fame a few years back when she convinced the Ohio legislature to expand the state university system. It was getting her great press.

"You know, Millie, it's fantastic what you've done with this."

"Thank you," she answered, formal.

"One day you should run for President," he teased.

"Only after you run your full eight years," she replied, seriously. "Nobody can beat you. You are too handsome."

"I'm not kidding, you know."

"Neither am I."

The windows suddenly blew open and a gust of wind swept the velvet curtains over his desk. Millicent's notes fluttered on the carpet. In seconds, the room became gray and muggy.

"Funny," the first lady murmured looking beyond the dark sky and the first drops of rain that settled on the exposed mahogany. "Talking like this reminds me..."

Without a word, Stone took her in his arms.

She resisted at first but then she let her head fall on his shoulder. He stroked her hair.

"Mill?" He pulled her chin up and looked her in the eyes. They were pale blue, guarded, surrounded by a web of worry. "You look lovely today." He tried to wipe her tears with his thumb.

"No I don't. I look like good old Millie."

He spent the rest of the morning exuberant. He missed Kay. He kept postponing the moment he'd call her, but he couldn't stop himself from racing to the phone every time his private line rang.

At 3 pm sharp he went to The Library determined to tell Kimberly she'd have to forget about him. He found her crying.

"You're never here for me, angel, you don't want to play with your Kimberly anymore."

Stone was speechless. They never had scenes. Theirs was an uncomplicated deal. They were both after one thing, and feelings were not part of it. Tears? Not with Kimberly! Today, of all days, he wanted her happy.

He spoke gently, explaining how hard the latest presidential business had been on him. But he knew that only one thing would calm her. She needed to know he still wanted her. So they fucked.

He laid back as always and let Kimberly do the things that pleased her, astride on his belly, congratulating himself on his stamina. He closed his eyes and marveled at how strange and different this all felt. How curious. A large blond woman was giving him the mechanics of pleasure. A little thrill, an edge of relief. Sex as fast food. Instant gratification without consequence. Pleasure abandoned his body as quickly as it came, leaving behind a sore back and the urge to wash. None of the inexplicable joy he carried with him ever since he and Kay first touched.

He kissed Kimberly fondly, then strode out the door, keen to get on with his afternoon appointments, keen to check his desk for a message from Kay.

None had come.

* * *

"He's getting laid somewhere else,"

Kimberly muttered as she paced furiously.

"He's getting it elsewhere or worse, he's fallen in love with someone else." Who?

There were no women around him that she had any reason to worry about. Unless it was Millicent who was claiming him back. "Well Millie," she said to herself, "You had your chance and now is my turn. I want this man. This man is spoken for."

The signs all pointed to another lover.

He was tender today, which he never was before. Bob loved hard sex, no foreplay. And he never closed his eyes before — not ever! He liked to watch. What the hell! And where had he been all this time? She'd have to find out what was going on.

Kimberly looked at her watch.

Dammit, she had to lecture at a drug rehabilitation symposium in an hour. She checked herself again in the glare of the French doors. Her bustier was tight and she looked fat. She popped a downer and two diet pills. She'd have to lose five pounds before the next time. Then he'd like her better. He'd like her enough to open his eyes.

But what if she was too old and ugly after all? What if he really didn't want her anymore? What if he wanted to dump her? She took the Ming vase she had bought him last Christmas and threw it at her reflection in the window. The glass barely quivered but the vase broke in tiny fragments and rose petals spread everywhere at her feet. She bent to pick them up when a sliver of porcelain pierced her skin.

"Damn you Bob!" she whispered, sucking the blood that gushed from her finger. "I won't let you do this to me."

* * *

Langley, Virginia

"It's perfect. How did you do it?" Jim Lennox asked, looking around the sixth floor conference room.

It was different from the rest of the building. Oval and opulent, with a 12 foot ceiling, maple molding and a wall of oak bookcases with a skinny spiral stepladder leading to a roped upper level. A set of large lampshades the color of raw silk cast a warm glow over the mahogany table, set for ten, where the CIA division heads would soon meet. Lennox caressed the back of his hand carved chair and turned to Beatrice.

"Don't ask what chits I called in for these two hours. This is your moment, Jim," his lieutenant said proudly.

"Not just my moment, Bea. Ours. Containment's. It's been a long time since senior management gave us the time of day."

His voice trailed off as he caught sight of Carson, the head of Intelligence, and his two assistants as they entered. He turned to greet them.

"Mr. Carson. Gentlemen. Thank you for coming on such short notice."

Carson shook his hand absently.

"Not at all, Jim, not at all." He cast his eyes quickly on the empty seats arranged evenly around the table. His pale, gray face showed an uneasiness that worried Lennox.

He had just begun introducing Beatrice to Carson's staff when Converse of Clandestine Operations walked in accompanied by Wade Jennings. What was he doing there? Jennings was an active operative — the only man in the room who had spent his life in the field.

"Assistants behind seniors, please, and make it snappy. Time is short," Carson muttered loud enough for Beatrice to rush Converse to his seat and pull four chairs for the assistants in an improvised second row. The old man stood until everyone was settled and then, nodding his approval to Lennox, he sat.

"A few days ago you each received a comprehensive report on the new presidential nominee, Catherine Kemeny," Lennox started, taking a sip of coffee from a frail, blue cup. Beatrice had scavenged all morning for the china set that belonged to Alan Dulles. "Boss," she had said when she dug it out from a cupboard, dusty and chipped, "the occasion demands."

"But, as I informed you," he continued, "we have more urgent business at this time."

All eyes were on him. Lennox tried to stay calm.

"Acting on our own initiative, we followed up the normal search with an exhaustive review of certain key cases. We found most of them were linked to Grigor Vorody."

He let the name sink in. From where he sat, Lennox could see clearly the horizon line in the naval oil hanging above Carson's head join the deep crease where his eyes met.

"Kemeny's just announced she's going to activate her pursuit of Vorody based on new leads," Carson said.

Lennox nodded.

"We presumed from this that her nomination would impact on the interests of the Agency. But let's take a look at the report."

Beatrice distributed photocopied pages.

Converse and Carson glanced at them briefly.

"Nothing we don't know here," Carson said, looking at his watch.

"I'm afraid there's more."

Beatrice took her seat at the opposite end of the table behind Jennings. She looked Lennox in the eyes, prompting him to speak.

"We deployed surveillance when Vorody's name came up in Kemeny's case load. And we discovered something rather extraordinary."

The rhythmic pounding of Carson's pen tapping on paper suddenly stopped. Converse lit a second cigarette, leaving the first one still glowing.

"The President, gentlemen, is sleeping with Kemeny. We have their first encounter on tape."

No sound disturbed the silence for a long moment, except the muted rap of the unhinged windowpane.

Beatrice pressed the start button on the cassette player she had pulled from under the table. First Kay Kemeny's voice and then the President's. Murmurs, sighs, whispered endearments filled the room.

When the tape ended, Lennox spoke again.

"This took place last night, at the Regency Excelsior."

Converse turned to Jennings, and whispered something to him, then looked up to Beatrice.

"For the next phase of discussion, we will excuse all assistants," he said and watched everyone in second row rise. Beatrice looked pleadingly at Lennox but he avoided her glance.

"My compliments to your division, Jim," Converse said when they were alone. "Good job." Lennox smiled.

"I think you ought to know what we've known for a long time, if we're to handle this properly."

He looked at Carson and Jennings.

"Vorody came over to us in the 70s, offering to be our agent. He was with KGB then, and he was also secret service chief for Hungary. He passed all the tests. He was cleared by Angleton personally. No one here liked the man, a brutal son of a bitch, the worst. But we didn't make him what he was, and we would have been damned crazy not to accept his offer." He motioned to Carson, who loosened his collar.

"We've had a lot of — well — input, into Vorody's activities in the ten years he worked for us as double agent. We had to feed him a lot of good information to maintain his position. And we had to sit on a lot of good information too, or Pavlov would have smelled rat. There was a lot of collateral damage among civilians and even some American agents."

Jennings whispered something in Converse's ear. He listened intently, then nodded. Carson gestured him to speak up.

70

"He defected to the United States in the late 80's. Of course, the public would never understand how we rewarded him with U.S. citizenship and full protection. Obviously, Congressional hearings are the last thing we need at this time. He can't be exposed, much less prosecuted.

"We tried to give Kemeny the hint when she asked us for leads in the past. But she didn't pick up. She's obsessed with him. We don't know if she's aware of this, but her father was one of his victims. This makes her a wild card. We were afraid that if we confided in her she'd go public. Now her career is at stake as well, so an approach at this stage is out of the question."

Lennox was stunned. This was much bigger than he had imagined. The KGB chief for Hungary a CIA mole for a whole decade?

"As for the President," said Carson, "he's never been responsive to our concerns. And now it's obvious we can't risk our nation's security on his pillow talk.

"Converse let's go over the battle plan."

"Jim," Converse said firmly, "you've got your assignment. Terminate the nomination without causing undue embarrassment to the President. And without a hint of Agency involvement".

Lennox took in a deep breath and rose.

"Thank you, gentlemen. I'll have a plan ready in forty-eight hours."

TEN

Wiesbaden, Germany

"Stay here. I've got to go in alone and see if they'll talk to me. Don't attract attention," Jacobi said to Stevie as he struggled out of the car.

Don't attract attention? Oh well. Stevie smiled and shook his head. Let him have his moment. After all, how often did a former Mossad get to bring an American drug agent to the CIA?

Through a thin curtain of rain he watched Jacobi enter a dirty gray apartment complex.

It was on another meridian of the same jungle that he had met Jacobi. Wall Street, in March. Rain poured on the asphalt for three days, making him long to end this surveillance and arrest the Syrian. Crowds of people everywhere, streets streaked yellow by the rush hour flood of taxis.

Stevie watched the lone black limousine across the street.

He was following him, hoping to meet his contacts. He wanted to feel the rush again, the fire warming him inside every time he nailed not just the ring leader but the whole network.

The Syrian got out of the car and went into an old office building. The chipped stained glass front door shuddered behind Stevie when he joined him at the mouth of the elevator. The yellow lit arrow pointed up and a rickety steel slider opened.

The Syrian went in first, followed by Stevie. The elevator doors started to close. And inside the still box, no motion. Just then a hand reached in and the doors burst open. A burly, distracted looking man carrying a sample case and a bright apologetic smile pushed his way in.

"Sorry," he murmured, folding his dripping umbrella.

The Syrian's shoulders stiffened.

Sensing suspicion, Stevie touched 5. The target touched 12. The salesman fumbled in his pocket for a business card, read it and hit the top floor.

Stevie got out at 5 and ran up the staircase. He was breathing hard when he reached the 12th floor.

"Always let your target choose first."

He turned and saw first the brown leather case and then the salesman stepping out of the shadow.

"Ezra Jacobi. Private investigator. And you are DEA — Vitt, last name Vitt, am I right? How do you call yourself — Steve? Steven?"

"Stevie."

The short, stubby man motioned him to a space behind the fire extinguisher.

"Sorry I messed you up in the elevator."

Stevie sized up the man in front of him.

"Where's the Syrian?" he finally asked.

"In 1575. The U.S. branch of the Arab bank that funnels money to the PLO."

"What are you doing here?"

"I'm on this case for the airline. You know. The jumbo jet that blew up two months ago."

He turned toward the slim ray coming from the emergency exit. His small mouth pursed inquisitively.

"Maybe I can help you? Maybe you can help me?"

Stevie soon discovered that Jacobi already knew what there was to know about the case. He knew that the Syrian was part of a drug dealing terrorist network working with CIA's blessing. He knew that the deal was to help them get the hostages out of Lebanon and in turn they'd let them trade drugs and arms through Europe and the Americas — providing they got some into Nicaragua for the Contras.

CIA protected the drug route for the Syrian. The key was Frankfurt. A courier carrying a suitcase with clothes in it would arrive at the airport. The suitcase would pass through all the checkpoints, and once in the luggage handlers' area be exchanged by a terrorist plant with an identical suitcase loaded with drugs.

Except one day the Syrian brought a bomb in the suitcase. "They never thought the terrorists would lose such a sweet deal," Jacobi told him when they knew each other better. "But when those unpredictable motherfuckers blew up 259 Americans in that jet, what could the Agency do? Confess?"

Forty-five minutes later, Jacobi knocked on the Volkswagen door, flanked by two men in their thirties, one blond, thin and British in tailored tweeds, the other dark and athletic, in black leather. "Meet Peter and Hans."

They went to the Trattoria, Peter and Hans's favorite restaurant.

"It felt tense in there" Jacobi said after their appetizers arrived, his face frozen in a cordial expression.

"That's because it was," Hans answered with a wide smile.

"They're just down the hall, doing God knows what. The few I've seen were real stomach turners. Here, try this, the artichoke is spectacular." He pointed to the antipasto tray. "Now they're in so deep they've gone over the wall. They own Justice, but they're still worried about Congress and all the media attention."

He ate as he spoke, gesturing gaily.

"But watch out, "Peter added. "They will not let you or anyone open the lid on their operations."

They were talking about Vorody. Peter and Hans knew why he couldn't be touched. Stevie watched them, dissecting their words and their gestures. Peter spoke with an American accent and British phrasing. They could be talking about the weather, except Peter kept his focus on Stevie. And Hans's eyes never left Jacobi. They were talking about the Cowboys here. But what kind of business did the Cowboys have with Vorody? Was it sanctioned by Langley or were they running this on their own?

"I know they don't want anyone to get to the bottom, but this time it's inevitable." Jacobi said. "Too many people are looking. You're not the only ones. Lots of them want to clean house."

"The upper levels don't want to hear about house cleaning."

Hans's green eyes shifted for the first time to Stevie's.

"Stay away from Wiesbaden. Keep a low profile in Frankfurt. If they figure out what you're looking for we will not — repeat, not — be able to help."

Peter looked up at the waiter who breezed past to assure them the pasta was on its way.

"One of our men dropped out," he said, when they were alone again. "He's in hiding now and took some files. I'll try to arrange a meeting."

"But that's as far as we'll go."

"What do you think about the French elections?" Hans's asked suddenly when the main course arrived.

When they finished eating, Jacobi said, "I just want the passport, and any files you can get your hands on. I don't need anyone to testify. My friend here is not taking on the whole outfit."

"Is that true?" Peter asked Stevie.

"I just need what it takes to find him." He looked over to Hans. "And this meeting never happened."

"He lives in the U.S., with papers." Hans said, cautiously. "We are sure of that. Our man can help with the rest."

Peter threw Stevie a piercing glance.

"Tell me, do you think this lady lawyer can take it?"

"She's tough," Stevie said in an even voice.

"And the President is backing her up."

* * *

Minutes after the four men left the Trattoria the maitre d' pulled a cassette from the tape deck hidden in his office behind the store room and dialed a Frankfurt number.

"We had a visit from our American patrons today."

* * *

She called.

As the President walked back into his office Kay Kemeny called, oblivious to his guilt.

Stop being a child, he admonished himself. She'll never know about Kimberly.

He sounded cold at first, distant, until he whispered, "I missed you all day."

They met again that night, after his wife retired to her quarters in their ambiguously divided apartment upstairs. Millicent seemed warmer than usual, as if their momentary closeness had changed something. Stone caught himself fearing that she might want to rekindle the past. Not now Millie, he pleaded with her silently. Not now.

Kay didn't want to come to the White House at first, but he persuaded her it was the only way. How could he justify going to her hotel again without arousing suspicion? They agreed to meet at midnight in The Library.

Moments before the grandfather clock struck twelve times, it occurred to him that the maid would not yet have changed the bed linen in that room until the next day. He opened the door with his access card, not sure what he was going to say.

She was by the window, her tall, beautiful body covering with its shadow the damp spot Kimberley's broken vase had left on the Oriental rug. The bed was freshly made, and the vase replaced, filled to the brim with fresh evening roses.

Kay was nervous. Was this a one night stand?

Nothing could be right about their liaison. Even as a one night stand their night together was probably being dissected by Secret Service. To say nothing of the scrutiny they would undergo if they continued to see each other privately. Nothing was right about the wife and son sleeping upstairs. Nothing was right about her sacrificing her integrity as a professional. For the first time in her life, she was sleeping with the boss. For the first time in her life, she was sleeping with a married man. Nothing was right about this except that she was in love.

If Kay didn't already know it, she knew it when she saw him, beaming with a joy so singular that he seemed completely changed. They made love again, better it seemed, though that was not possible, longer certainly, taking time to explore their bodies.

"We're going to have to talk," Kay broke the calm silence.

"I know. I thought about it all day."

My God, he's going to say it's over, she thought, withdrawing from him.

"I can't stop seeing you," he said, looking away. "I don't want to get into my life's story, but I've never, ever felt this way before."

He spoke of how they would meet, each day before midnight. They could spend about two hours together without raising suspicions. Stone rarely slept more than five hours and always came back downstairs to work after Millicent said good night. It was not enough, he knew. He'd have Roger walk her the few blocks to her hotel, since cars would be checked exiting the White House. Roger knew a secret way.

He sounded so expert at deceit she couldn't help wondering about his past adventures. She had heard a rumor that there had been something between Stone and Kimberly Devane. She could hardly believe that this magnificent lover could find anything remotely attractive in the chubby Texas debutante.

Everything about their illicit rendezvous in that bachelor pad made Kay feel awkward. Embarrassed. She had never been the second woman in a man's life. She had never had to hide before. She didn't know what to make of the contradictory thoughts that passed through her mind. But Stone made love to her again, and everything was forgotten. As the sun rose on their last good-bye, he said, "We'll have to be more careful next time. You must always leave before daylight."

* * *

Maybe before politics, before the presidency, it would have been different. Now, despite Clancy Leduc's long tirade about her husband having a love affair with the human rights nominee, she did not worry. She knew Bob like she knew herself. He couldn't stand being loved by just one woman. He wanted all of humanity.

Millicent paced her office, situated directly across from her husband's, in the opposite wing of the White House. Her family portraits, six generations of Pembertons, three of them governors, one senator, lined the walls in controlled harmony. A meticulously arranged Murano menagerie from her grandmother's collection decorated a Florentine coffee table.

Love. How perfectly childish of Leduc to mistake for love another of Bob Stone's short and passing attacks of sensuality.

"Joan," she said in the interphone. "Ask Mr. Leduc to join me."

* * *

Langley, Virginia

Gene Boren welcomed the opportunity to smear President Stone's favorite nominee.

The small, fine-boned man in the gray cubicle carefully wiped the dust off his desk, cleared his computer screen and leaned back in his chair, hands supporting his painful neck. Fifteen years at Containment, fifteen years in front of a computer were enough to destroy a man's posture and make him depend on every kind of New Age therapy. He rubbed a greasy yellow potion on the sensitive spot below his hairline, and reached for a Kleenex. Damn. Who the hell was taking his stuff all the time?

He closed his eyes and tried to put everything else but Kemeny out of his mind. His thin lips pursed and he whistled faintly. Tchaikovsky's *Petite Russie*. His work was like that — complex, all-encompassing. A veritable symphony.

His mind rolled back the recording of Kemeny's encounter with the President. This was a welcome challenge. He looked forward to finding her Achilles heel, to handing her nomination over to Lennox on a platter, along with a foolproof plan that would get Congress to reject her. Lately things hadn't been exactly exciting at Containment.

Fifteen years ago he had joined the CIA figuring it was the perfect cure for his ambiguous sexuality. He planned to immerse himself in danger and forget about his unsettling desires. He wanted to be safely surrounded by strong, straight, unshakable men. Instead he discovered an entire underground of homosexual CIA men, strong and unshakable, but gay nevertheless. They socialized at a well guarded club, in complete secrecy. Among them, bonds were stronger than in any other Intelligence faction. They needed one another to survive.

Leading an otherwise solitary life, Gene loved to solve intelligence riddles and to discuss them in the basement of the Queen's Regiment. So that night he stopped at the club to see if anyone there knew about Kemeny and, in particular, about this former KGB she was chasing, a man whose name he had, surprisingly, never heard before. Grigor Vorody.

* * *

Virginia

Wade Jennings was not comforted by the Domestic Containment assignment. Sure, they thought Gene Boren was their man to handle the Kemeny affair but he sensed that more needed to be done.

At 53, Jennings looked 10 years older. On his puffy, rugged face, unsightly veins and creases mapped what had been by any standards an impossible life for a man who was neither a saint nor the devil incarnate. Thirty years with the job, at Clandestine Operations during which he had seen too much, heard too much, ignored too much.

He looked at the Kemeny file with the remarkable Vorody annotations as he had looked twenty years ago at a stack of photos and histories of CIA's native agents in Hungary. The name Vorody flashed at him from that file, tormenting him with the horror of what he had done.

He could never forget the day he was told to pick from those pictures and life stories the ones who would be sacrificed to ensure that double agent Grigor Vorody continued his rise to the top in the Hungarian faction of KGB. He remembered begging Racklee to let him off the hook. He was just a man, how could he be expected to play God? "The selection is preliminary. The ball doesn't stop at you," Racklee told him. "There are others who will have a crack at these names." Sure enough, the men he picked all got killed or worse, thrown in a Soviet jail.

And now, could they afford to have the Vorody story in the open simply to preserve the life of a nominee?

No. Boren might be the right man but he, Wade Jennings, was not going to rely on him to offset the debacle. Jennings knew that he would ultimately resort to Racklee. How did he know Racklee wasn't on the job already? He must have heard Kemeny mouthing off about her "Inquisitor" on every channel. Who says that Racklee, or for that matter Vorody himself, weren't out there doing their own damage control? Jennings shuddered.

If he called on Racklee now he would be as responsible as the killer himself. And he would find himself in the middle of everything.

This Vorody business sounded as bad as the Iran Contra affair. Worse. And he really didn't think his career, let alone his health, could withstand another one of those. For fifteen years he had taken on nearly irreconcilable duties. After CIA's Director threw out Racklee and his Cowboys in 1978, Jennings was made CIA contract officer to Racklee for approved off-the-books activities. He also worked for Racklee directly, as his unofficial CIA facilitator, sourcing for him CIA's top secret files. Thanks to this set up, Racklee knew more, and had more power now than he did when he was inside the system.

So, if he screwed up with the Agency, the Agency would fire him without a pension. If he screwed up with Racklee, he wouldn't have to worry about a pension at all.

* * *

Camp Peary, USA, 1954

"Welcome to The Farm."

The young boy stretched his neck to see behind the rugged young lieutenant who introduced himself as code-name Forest.

"This is the camp for secret operatives. Here no one has a name, or a past. Just a number. Yours is 151. As in your age — 15 and one month exactly."

The Farm was nothing more than four white buildings with small squares for windows, spread evenly among patches of dead grass and surrounded by an obstacle course. Behind them loomed a kind of outdoor dump, a long stretch of uneven, battered land, designed most likely for field training activity.

Forest handed the new trainee a green metal box.

"For personal effects. After you fill it, you must leave it here with me."

He took off his black cap and a crown of flame red hair burst out, like poppy.

He put the cap on the rookie's head. The wide rim covered the boy's brown eyes. But the boy did not move. He kept his green box high and his lips tight.

The lieutenant pushed the cap back and gave 151 a firm pat on the back.

"It's OK, kid. This cap was once too big for me."

ELEVEN

The Inquisitor pulled a tin army box from his desk. It was scratched, old, overflowing with the past. On top, just where he had left them, were photos of Catherine Kemeny as a little girl. Strawberry red lips, shaped exactly like a heart. Thick, golden curls. Pity. Her hair had turned so dark lately. His fingers traveled over the last belongings of Nicholas Kemeny.

He leafed through a small batch of newspaper clippings and university transcripts he had collected over the years. She did well, Nicholas's girl. His eyes, brown and quiet, rested on the pale face.

Why him?

Of all his victims, why had he grown so close to Kemeny? And when exactly was it that the mementos of another man's life had become his own?

From outside, he heard thunder. The room suddenly darkened, wrapping him in a thick curtain of tropical rain.

The rain that fell against the 20-inch window in the cell he shared with the girl's father had been different. It was autumn rain, the kind of dirty, inexplicable rain that fell only in Hungary. The prison was nothing like Lubyanka. It was smaller, uglier. It was there that he did time with Nicholas Kemeny.

Nicholas was already sick when Grigor became his cellmate. He knew then, at 35 years of age, that those zebra striped clothes were the last he'd ever feel on his body.

Grigor played a doctor this time, jailed for performing an abortion. Abortions were illegal in communist Hungary. So was publishing anti-communist books abroad. That's why Kemeny was there. Grigor's assignment was to find out who smuggled the manuscripts and how the Western publishers were contacted. Kemeny had been tortured for almost a year but would not talk. So Grigor became Kemeny's friend.

"I'm only here a few more weeks. I did the rest of my time in hard labor camp. But I was transferred to Budapest to be closer to my wife. She's having a child," Grigor tells him when they are at ease with each other. He's been there more than two weeks and wants to get out soon. The water that streams down the corridors, filled with feces, sluggish and brown, makes him sick. At home, he has a large stark bedroom with fresh blue sheets and a large blonde maid who gives him relief.

"Do you want me to do anything for you when I'm out?"

"See my daughter and my wife for me. Tell them I love them. Don't tell them what's been done to me."

"I see you write all the time. Could I —"

"Don't even think it. You've got a chance to get out and mind your own life."

"I don't think I can. Not after I've seen you. Not after this."

"Don't. Get out. Live. Just live."

The next day Nicholas lets him take a look at his pages. There's a book there, a whole book under that mattress. Just a chapter or two to finish.

"What a pity it would be for this to be destroyed," Grigor tells him, and he means every word. "Please trust me. Tell me how to do it and I'll get your book out of here. I promise."

Another week. More pain. Nicholas comes back without fingernails. He bleeds over his pages so he dictates a chapter to Grigor. Grigor writes. The guards come again and take Nicholas away. Grigor is bitten by a rat. He complains and gets a bandage and a tetanus shot. They keep Nicholas out of the cell until it's done. In ice-cold water over his knees because he has white feet and shivers for two days when he gets back. That night, Grigor gives him his blanket.

Nicholas dictates now to Grigor all the time. The nail trick worked, even though it was so old no one used it anymore. Nicholas trusts Grigor. No one comes to take his pages away.

"I have three more days in here," Grigor announces after he comes back from a visit with his wife. He has another medical book with him to study. "We have to keep up with what's going on in our field."

Nicholas starts to talk. He tells him all about his contacts. He writes feverishly all night to finish the last chapter. His fingers are better. He writes and writes. He dots the last sentence. The end. That night Grigor watches him begin to die.

The next day he reports to his superiors. Mission accomplished. The contacts are arrested and taken in for interrogation. He can pack.

"We'll give him the RAD full force now. We don't want him walking out of here alive."

The RAD is as bad as Hiroshima. It comes through the chair, in the interrogation room. They know the longer they sit in that chair the sooner they die. It's all in the open. They are told. They rot inside. They cook inside. Many talk even before they turn the damned thing on. Nicholas is not one of those.

"Why kill him now?" he hears himself ask. "There's nothing more he can say now. Keep him alive and I'll see he never steps out of line. He's got enough RAD to die within a year."

He does this. Why? He asks for trouble, he causes suspicion, he sees it in his superior's eye.

They seat Nicholas on that chair one more time.

He watches Nicholas die. He cannot leave him now. He decides to stay until the end.

"Take care of Catherine if you get out of this alive," is all he keeps asking.

"You'll be all right, Nicholas. You will come out, you'll see." His words are so far from the truth that they sound foreign. Chinese.

"Don't lie to me."

Nicholas tries to cheat his regret.

"Life has been long enough for me. I'm no good anymore now. I've played my part. I'm tired, I'm spent. I couldn't write anymore, I lost — I lost my memory." His voice speaks from afar. He has started crossing the threshold but is still suspended in this world. "I can't remember the way home from the bridge, for example. How many streets to the left, or is it to the right? How many? Or how you say 'I love you' in Italian. I can't remember."

Grigor wants to tell him that his life, too, seems long enough.

"Ti amo," he says instead. "That's how you say I love you in Italian. I don't know about getting home from the bridge. But you're on Franz Liszt, and that's just three blocks from the university."

"I know all about death," Grigor begins that last day. "I killed many."

The autumn wind is moaning outside and Nicholas is yellow and drawn. He grows paler still. His lips are white. He whispers.

"Who are you?"

"I am the son of Sandor Vorody."

"But you're a doctor. Aren't you?"

"No."

Nicholas mouths the words in a sort of trance.

"You are the son of the communist, Sandor Vorody... You did this — to me?"

The voice has no ring to it anymore. No timbre. Just the lips moving, uttering words. Grigor knows what they'd be.

"I had to. For our cause. I'm working for the other side. Do you believe me?"

They say dying men grow alert one more time, before the spirit leaves them. He hopes that time is now. He asks again, holding Nicholas's head high, demands an answer.

"Do-you-believe-me?"

The words come back quickly, with shocking clarity.

"Take care of Catherine and Mary."

Grigor is relieved. He is amazed at how light he feels all of a sudden, how free. Telling the truth. What bliss. Catharsis. The unexpected gift seems more important than forgiveness. It makes him anxious to continue. To share. Where to begin? With Pavlov? With Racklee? His words come out in torrents, unleashed, unveiling page by page the most fearsome chapter in cold war history.

But it is all too late for Nicholas Kemeny.

* * *

Miami, Florida

Games. They think he had time for their games.

Edwin Forest Racklee shook his head warily at the prospect of another Containment plan. Probably a nice, efficient, micro-managed plan. With some luck — something the Agency had to count on these days — they'd draw Kemeny into a game that would destroy her. But his man Jennings was too smart to count on Containment. And so was he.

He snorted in disgust and stood up to his full 6' 2". At 65, the 100 sits ups, 100 push ups, 50 pull ups and 15 minutes of Khata Yoga each morning kept him as trim and hard as he was at 40. Only today he felt a lot meaner. His leonine head framed by a crown of red wavy hair showed only the faintest traces of gray. High cheekbones sharpened by time set off a determined mouth with dry, pale lips. Wild brows the color of cayenne made his black eyes deeper, darker, like pokers. Something about those eyes, something about that face, carved irreversibly in smileless pose, made Edwin Forest Racklee look like an alien.

It was another blinding day of South Florida sunshine when he took the car out to the Sandy Beach Motel for his breakfast of fried eggs, sliced steak and toast. He went there regularly ever since Martha stopped cooking his meals. Over breakfast he made it a point to remember her as she was before her illness. For one moment each day Martha was alive and looking at him.

He seldom returned to the same place with any kind of pattern, a habit of training more than anything, because nowadays Racklee was not in danger from anyone.

But the Sandy Beach Motel was an exception. It was a rundown tourist haunt in Miami Beach, populated by a transient crowd, in which you never saw a face twice. The waitress only spoke Basque, a kind of Spanish that even the local Cubans couldn't understand. They pointed and gestured a lot. From his seat, he could see in every direction all the way to the horizon, and the food was as passable here as in any other place on the no man's land that stretched between Ocean Drive and Millionaires' Row.

Gesturing to the waitress to bring the usual, Racklee took his place on the broken deck. An ocean breeze blew above and a hungry seagull stopped on the frail railing, pecking at a forgotten fish bone, just an inch or two away from his hand. The railing shuddered under its weight. He moved his hand and watched the bird fly away.

The crest of a wave touched his foot and with it, a memory.

"Congratulations, major, the implant was perfect." Donovan shakes his hand and gives him a white envelope.

"Now we have to turn 151 into Pavlov's right hand."

Silently, he reads the instructions.

"The boy, you understand, is too good to keep just for Hungary."

Racklee is proud. He trained 151 to defend the American Century.

It's not easy to find the kind of subterfuge that would bring him right into Pavlov's grace. But he does. Jennings brings him the answer. Two American agents working on a plot to overthrow the government in Hungary. High-powered Hungarian generals ready to turn the army against the centralized government and take over with American help. It's hopeless and everyone at Langley knows it, including the agents. But they also know it can come in handy.

151 uncovers the plot. He exposes the generals and the agents.

But it's not enough. Still no word from Pavlov. 151 gets a promotion with the Hungarian Secret Service. In Dallas and Missouri, two wives and five children are left with two small metal jars wrapped in a star spangled banner inscribed Pro Patria Mori.

He sends a newsman born in Budapest back to Hungary to film a documentary. Jennings gives him times and places to meet and interview dissidents in Leningrad, Bucharest and Prague. He tells him to wait for a sign at the Hotel Intercontinental when he's ready. 151 gets there at dawn and takes him in. The footage goes first to the KGB. The man is found cold as ice in a bag of dirty laundry. A telegram and a decoration come from Pavlov. Pro Patria Mori.

There's word at Langley of an uprising in the gold mines of Transylvania. It will happen on the visit of the Hungarian and Romanian prime ministers. The miners will take them hostage and make demands. Food on their tables, oxygen masks, early retirement, higher salaries, freedom to travel to the West, freedom to speak. For real, not just constitutionally. 151 is sent to accompany the prime minister of Hungary. Deep in the mines, they are taken hostage. 151 and his squad have masks, poison gas and sharp weapons. He retires all the miners. He rescues the delegation. The press mentions nothing.

Pavlov finally calls.

He asks 151 to play double agent with the CIA.

Bartlett is deployed to arrange contact with Angleton. Bartlett knows nothing more about 151 than that he's KGB and wants to turn CIA. By now Donovan is gone. So is Dulles. All files on the implant are destroyed. No one knows about 151 being trained at Camp Peary. No one but his mentor, Edwin Forest Racklee.

James Jesus Angleton takes a personal interest in 151 from the start. By now he's paranoid and he drinks. He thinks of nothing but moles and implants. He believes nothing and no one. He goes at 151 much harder than the KGB.

They feed him what he wants. People die. Again. Children. Russians. Palestinians. Airplanes fall. Weapon shipments are apprehended. Terrorists are killed in the act. When 151 makes it through the debriefing, he tells Racklee it was easy, because everything he says to Angleton about turning to the Americans is true. His father's truth, only packaged differently. After he passes the test 151 sends his report to Pavlov. Three words. Jesus loves me.

One year later 151 makes it to secret service chief. All of Hungary's business is under his command. He creates the world's finest disinformation ministry. And he reports directly to Pavlov. He is Pavlov's channel to the CIA, the most important piece of the Eastern intelligence puzzle.

"Yes," Racklee murmured between clenched teeth, drowning a bothersome wasp in a bath of honey. The insect struggled in the golden clay, losing one by one its wings, then its feet. "We've lost many. But in the end the two of us destroyed the KGB."

There are two ways to arrange the defection: one is to have 151 disappear from a major city in Europe where, as head of the Hungarian secret service, he travels freely. But that's too simple, too straightforward. Not humiliating enough.

151 brings the answer. He will disappear at sea. He will be missing for 30 days, accidentally. But before he goes, he places a slow-acting virus in the KGB computer matrix. It's programmed to gradually ravage all data. Misassigning codes, passwords, addresses and names, scrambling games, maddening and dangerous enough to have agents kill other agents. Everyone distrust everyone else. So it does. Vorody's virus becomes the ultimate disinformation weapon turned against disinformation itself.

He sees the KGB contact people with codes that no longer mean anything. Worse, they contact the wrong people. He sees them placing an order with a civilian indicating times and places for operations tied to names of agents who will pay with their lives. Sending millions of dollars into the wrong accounts, shipping weapons to the wrong ports, offering to trade drugs with the local schoolteacher, jeopardizing everyone's security long before they know 151 left for good. 151 was right. If he had left the normal way, Pavlov would have known immediately that their entire intelligence was in jeopardy. First Racklee has to watch them crawl. When he is done, 30 days passed, the operations worldwide nearly destroyed, he gives Pavlov the second blow. 151 defected and he is spilling his guts to the Americans. No longer just a casualty of the Black Sea.

And then comes the last announcement. 151 was a CIA implant from the start.

Racklee felt an exquisite shiver of pleasure travel down his spine. The unforgettable day when the report read not just that KGB, but the entire Soviet Union had crumbled.

He had lived to see the end of the secret network of Russian spies and agents he had battled all his life.

When he left, 151 took with him Russian intelligence. Behind him the doors closed on KGB.

He neither heard nor saw the approach of the man who now stood tall in front of him, his body angled directly in the sun, making him look indistinguishable, like a giant ink spot. The man was less than a foot from him but Racklee still couldn't make out his face. He blinked, and panicked for a moment.

"Greetings, code-name Forest. Remember me?"

Racklee's brows lifted imperceptibly.

"How could I forget you, Vorody.

"But this is not smart. And it's your third major fuck up since you landed here."

The chair creaked under Racklee's back. His neck strained to look up at the tall man, and his eyes ached from the sun which had shifted again and was burning his pupils. "First the two pigeons which put you in the mess you're in today. Now you meeting me."

"May I join you?"

Grigor sat next to Racklee without waiting for an answer. He closed his eyes and took a deep breath, savoring, it seemed, the morning sun.

"You know, Lieutenant," he murmured, "this smell, the salt — you're right about this place. It's blessed here."

"The woman had to go and you should have taken care of her," Racklee barked unhappily. "Everything about her was damn risky. Only you had approval on exit visas in Hungary. And what do you do when she starts singing? You leave her to me."

Grigor's pupils quivered.

"And your man Jonas wrote your name on his papers at that convention before you took him out. The asshole. He wrote I SAW GRIGOR VORODY."

Grigor opened his eyes.

"He paid too, didn't he?"

Moments passed. The silence, heavy with apprehension, was pierced only by the hungry cries of seagulls.

"Too many of those damned birds here today," Racklee said, unexpectedly.

"So what do you want now, Vorody?"

"I expect you to stop Kemeny immediately."

Racklee followed the birds with his eyes as they stormed around the shore dizzily.

"I expect you to do that for everyone's sake, not just me. It's bad enough that I've been recognized twice. We have too much at stake. You, me, and your Agency." Anger started to color Vorody's voice. "Keep her out of our life or you'll be up to your neck in mine, Racklee."

The Lieutenant lifted his heavy shoulders from the wicker, letting his body fall forward, looking straight into his pupil's eyes.

"Consider her out."

Grigor sank back into his chair.

"How?"

"Containment has a plan — they want to force her to resign."

"If it doesn't work?

"If it doesn't, they leave her to me. But I have to let them try and straighten this out their own way. They want alternatives, but not the final kind. They are afraid of publicity."

Grigor turned to the Basque waitress and asked for tea in her native tongue. A question mark rose high in Racklee's eyes.

"Come now, Forest. Don't be surprised. I learned everything there was to learn. You taught me."

Grigor's hand moved toward his breast pocket. He was dressed in black and his forehead, pale and clear, stayed dry despite the blistering heat.

"Slow down," warned Racklee.

"Don't worry, Lieutenant. You know not to worry."

His hand seemed empty when he brought it out of the hidden place where the tiny package of film had nested. He placed it carefully at the bottom of Racklee's empty cup.

"Here are my memories."

"And the original?"

"With my insurance agency."

The tea arrived in time to break the tension. Vorody placed three teaspoons of sugar in the boiling liquid and watched them melt.

"And that's not all," he continued, suddenly.

"It's not?"

"I want Kemeny out of the way or I'll have even bigger cards to play."

Sweat trickled down Racklee's face, tickling the edge of his nostrils, making him queasy. He took an ice cube from his water and crushed it against his cheeks.

"All right then." he murmured and wiped his face dry, slowly. "You can count on me."

Racklee didn't have to ask what was on the piece of film that lay innocently at the bottom of a dirty cup inscribed I - heart - Miami. He placed it carefully in his shirt pocket. Just an inch-long strip of celluloid carrying within it the essence of the cold war, The Inquisitor's story. The story of a 15-year-old boy who was given over to the CIA by his father, to be turned into the perfect monster of the KGB. The perfect triple agent who devoted his life to America, in whose name, with whose blessing, and at whose urging he performed for twenty-five years the most horrible deeds known to man. The stories of so many lives, and so many deaths. A small, poignant reminder of how fragile was the giant power of the CIA. An insignificant piece of film, subject to a mugger who might tear it away at gunpoint right now as Racklee opened his car door, to a paramedic who might find it if a heart attack or a truck struck him on the way, to the rescue team that might find it in the debris if a hurricane ravaged his home.

Subject, more likely, to Containment's failure to terminate the nomination of Kay Kemeny.

Racklee still held Vorody's testament in his hand when he placed his call to Jennings. They would not breathe a word to the President. But Converse needed to know that Vorody was out of hiding and threatening to expose them. The head of Clandestine Operations must be told at least part of the truth. That, if he was not protected, Vorody would take everything and everyone with him.

"Games," Racklee repeated, this time with a much heavier burden on his mind. "Games the little faggots at Containment think they can afford to play. Some kind of smear campaign."

He decided he'd wait three more days. On the fourth, he'd have a plan in motion for Vorody.

TWELVE

Kay woke up to the roar of Manhattan. How she had missed the city! Her apartment, at the top of one of Central Park West's old deco buildings, was large and airy. She inherited it from Uncle Daddy after he died.

Her uncle's real name was Daniel, Danny to his friends, but when she was little he liked to throw her in the air, dancing with her to the tune of Strauss's *Blue Danube*, so she would laugh and scream for more. Uncle Daddy, Uncle Daddy, please don't stop. Uncle Daddy. She was too young to pronounce her N's. So the name stuck. His friends and colleagues all called him Daddy, so much so that everyone eventually forgot his real name.

Uncle had once been a principal ballet dancer in Hungary, whose career was cut short by a two-year prison sentence for homosexuality. By then she was 8 years old and plagued by nightmares from which she awakened screaming, drenched in sweat.

After his release, Uncle Daddy was changed. He spent most of his time locked away in the dark library of their house, listening to music and making notes no one could understand.

Then they put Nicholas in jail.

After he died there, Mother and Uncle planned their escape. Nicholas's friends got them what they needed to cross the border into Austria: money, a map with the unchecked border points marked in red ink, and contact with a guide who would take them up to the mine field. From there, they would be on their own. If they were caught, death would come painfully, from beatings and starvation, in a communist prison. "We'll pray for freedom first," said Mother," and if we can't have that, we'll pray for a land mine."

They crossed the border on their elbows and knees, covered in white wool blankets that smelled of sheep and warm country stoves, inching ever so lightly on the thick snow.

Their faces, clothes and shoes were all painted white, invisible as they advanced, like moving dunes on the endless glistening surface.

Two hundred feet from the border they paused to catch their breath, intoxicated by the nearness of freedom.

It was Kay's mother who first saw the young, red-faced patrol guard perched above them. He lifted Kay's blanket with the tip of his rifle.

"Hands up," he yelled. Kay started crying.

"I'm taking you in."

Mother knelt at his feet, hugging his boots.

"Soldier, let us go and you can have anything we've got. Our money, our clothes, take everything."

The man stood tall above her and grinned: "I'll take it all anyway, bitch." He kicked Mother hard in the stomach. "You'll have to kill us," she managed to whisper.

"Sure I do. You think I want to spend Christmas filing reports? You think I'm going to turn in your stuff when I have a family at home, hungry kids, not like you bitches with your gold rings and watches."

Kay could smell vodka on his breath.

"You fucking traitors."

He cocked his shotgun and pointed it at her.

Kay looked at her mother and saw defeat in her face. If she didn't do something quickly she would never see her again.

"Run!" she cried. She got up and pushed the soldier away with all her might. Surprised by the attack, he turned the back of his shotgun and smashed it against the child's face with a loud crack. Blood spurted from her head, coloring the snow around them purple red, spraying their white painted faces and the white clothes and blankets. There was a scream. Someone was screaming. Blinded by her own blood, Kay couldn't see what was happening. They were being killed by the soldier. She crossed herself and waited for the sound of his gun. But there was silence. She felt Uncle Daddy lift her up in his arms and throw her over his shoulder. She heard Mother urging him to run. She buried her face in his shoulder. She could smell pine and spruce and the fireplace at home. She was warm again, as if a miracle had happened. It was Christmas! She fainted.

She woke up to the sound of her mother's voice speaking softly in German to a woman she had never seen before. "We're in Austria honey," Mother said. "We're safe. Everything will be all right now."

"Where's Uncle?"

"He's fine. He's with us. Sleep. Everything will be fine."

And the soldier? What had happened to him? How did they escape? Why didn't he shoot them? But she fell asleep before the words could form, and later, all Mother told her was that the soldier had gone away.

Twenty years later, hours before he fell into his last coma, she asked Uncle Daddy what really happened that day.

"I told you. The guard let us go. We lucked out. That's all."

But in her heart, she knew different. She knew that her mother, who would not hurt a fly, had stabbed that soldier with the hunting knife she had tied around her waist. Kay had seen her undo the holster and hold the handle tight. Somehow she could picture Mother slashing at him, instinctive and lethal. She could see her drop the knife in the snow and urge Uncle to run, leaving the man to die that cold Christmas night. She could see the snow behind them, drenched in their blood.

From the moment they arrived in New York, the three of them stayed together, first in a rundown apartment in Astoria where all immigrants went and then in the heart of bohemian Chelsea in Manhattan. They worked hard to put Kay through school, although they could not have done it without a generous grant from an anonymous benefactor. Perhaps a friend of Father's who had escaped before. She always wondered who it was.

Uncle staged and choreographed modern dance. Just as Kay was finishing college, he finally got his big break. They moved to the apartment on Central Park West, the most beautiful street in the city. Mom started working with crack children. Later, she moved in with them in a rehab center. She kept saying, "I've got so many children now. They all need me," every time Uncle asked her to take it easy. A few years later Uncle Daddy got ill with a mysterious illness and a year later he died in Mother's arms.

Now Mother lived in Florida and the apartment was all Kay's. Certain rooms still brought back the sound and scent of Uncle Daddy, the memory of another time, when the three of them were together, a happy, unconventional family.

In the large ornate bathroom which opened from the narrow stem of the main foyer, Kay stopped to look at herself in the mirror. She had changed in the past two weeks. Love and power altered her face. Her eyes seemed larger, luminous. Her scar, eternal reminder of their escape, seemed more important on this new face, more pronounced. She always believed it had magical powers. The doctors told her that it would fade as she grew older, but the scar did as it pleased. Almost invisible on the days when Kay was at peace, it flushed bright and fierce when she was restless or distraught.

Tony was home when she called him, surprised and happy she was back, even for just one evening. The President had asked her to join him for a public appearance at the artists/writers softball game in East Hampton the next day. He felt she would learn how to play the media better if she participated in their event.

"You couldn't have called me a day in advance? What if I have other plans?"

"If you have other plans I'll understand."

They went for dinner to Cafe des Artistes, just a few blocks from her home. It was a relief, in a way, to be with Tony, familiar and predictable, without the scrutiny and fear of being found, without the contradictions she felt ever since she had fallen in love with another man. Life with Tony felt so much more, well, manageable. Life after her affair with the President.

"He really has you following him around doesn't he?" Tony asked after they were seated.

"It's what presidents do with nominees."

"Yes, but you're special, aren't you. He'll have you at his side after you get confirmed too, am I right?"

"Not necessarily."

"I hear he likes women."

The Chassagne Montrachet came to her rescue and with it the maitre d' who congratulated her for her success on "Nightline".

"I'm going to East Hampton because he wants me to work the media better, be more friendly. Make them like me," she told Tony, knowing the diatribe this was likely to trigger, but willing to do anything to cut off discussion about Robert Stone.

Tony surprised her.

"He's right. They'll eat you alive if you don't. The confirmation is just the first step. You've got an entire lifetime to fight them afterwards."

She took his hand.

"Boy Kay, I wish you were a normal woman. Someone who doesn't fight against the world all the time."

"Do you really?"

"I'm tired of you playing their game."

"It's my life's work, Tony. I never hid it from you."

"Who cares, dammit, about history and politics? Why doesn't anyone give a damn about art and music and talent and culture in this fucking American No Mans Land?"

Tony's arched dark brows collided from the anger that twisted his pale high forehead into a knot. His beautiful lips twisted into an ugly grimace.

"Face it, Kay. Only your countrymen really give a damn about catching Vorody. The rest of America looks at it like it's some kind of an entertainment thing. A Chuck Norris flick. To them it's exciting, it's FUN."

Tony was talking too loudly. People were beginning to stare.

"You're the latest happening, babe. Hey, if I were you I'd quit politics and become a B-movie queen. After all you've still got great tits, even if you're past your prime. Let's ask Stone what he thinks about that."

She was afraid of what Tony would do if she spoke. She remained silent, looking down at her untouched plate, while Tony finished his meal.

He asked for the check and placed it near her. Here, pay it, the gesture said. You're the one who sold out.

"I thought you supported my career," she said, finally.

"I did," he replied. His voice quivered.

"When you still loved me."

* * *

Berlin, Germany

The old man was thin, bald, bent forward as if he was searching for something he dropped on the ground. The park bench was his. Spread on it, a brown paper bag, a small gray thermos, and a white paper napkin with a half bagel from whose center stuck the pink flesh of smoked fish.

He and Jacobi spoke a few words in Yiddish. Then Jacobi switched to English.

"This is my American friend, Stevie."

He nodded, looking up for a moment, then his eyes dropped.

"Nice shoes. I'm Shimon."

"Nice to meet you."

"You're looking for one of yours, then?"

"No, not one of ours." Stevie looked at Jacobi.

"We're looking for a former KGB."

"Oh." Shimon looked up again, straightening his body with a great effort. "I see."

He dug into the brown bag, wrinkling it with his fingers. The park was quiet and dark, still damp from the rain, and the dry paper made an unsettling noise. Was he dreaming or did he see in that bag the glimmer of a Beretta just like the one he'd seen on Jacobi?

"Here. Take this."

The old man handed him the corner of a napkin on which he could barely see a name and an address, scribbled in a shaky, uneven scrawl.

"Thank you."

Shimon shrugged and picked up his bagel. He took a vigorous bite, with white, sharp teeth, and squinted at the sun, whose first ray in days pierced the rock gray sky. He sighed and looked down again.

"Muddy business, this Grigor Vorody."

* * *

"Larry honey, where is that darling president of ours heading this weekend?" Kimberly asked her sleeping husband, that Friday night.

Devane had fallen asleep on the Turkish divan.

"What, Kimmie? Is that you?" Larry blinked and opened his eyes. "Is it morning yet?"

"No, sweetie, it's still Friday night. I just wanted to know where Stone went for the weekend."

"Who cares," Devane muttered, rubbing his eyes like a child with the back of his hand. His pale, thin hair was golden blond and his eyes, crystal blue, cut two sleepy slits on the pink, moon-shaped baby face. No wonder Leduc's nickname had stuck. "I'm here aren't I? I have to mind the ship while the commander is off having fun".

"Come on, go back upstairs. I'll join you in a while." He rolled away from her.

Kimberly shook him impatiently. He opened one eye again, begging for peace, but she was merciless tonight.

"I want to know if Millie's with him, 'cause if she's not I have a zillion things I have to catch up with her."

Defeated, Devane groaned and sat up.

"Millicent is gone too, but not with Stone. She's in San Francisco, I think."

"How about Bob?" she asked, and then smiled teasingly. "Where is he and why is he making my man work weekends?" She massaged his scalp and he purred.

"Uhmmmm...Kimmie, you have magic fingers..."

"So? Where's Bob?"

"New York."

"Whatever for?"

"Some writers shindig." Larry closed his eyes. "At the beach, in East Hampton."

Kimberly leaned against Larry's back, her large breasts pressing hard against his shoulder blades.

"You know, sweet," she murmured, "I think women are underestimated in this government. I mean, there's Millie and me, but heck Larry, there's really no one without a husband who brought her aboard. No one who counts. I thought we were going to get on with a whole new world, where there'll be lots of women running things. Isn't that right?"

"Well, there are a few."

"Yeah? Like who?"

"Well, there's Linda, the assistant to the Secretary of Commerce."

"She doesn't count, honey. Who else?"

"Lucy Minardi, the Italian girl who runs Health and Human Services under Rollins."

"She has no clout."

"There's Kay Kemeny, but of course, she's not confirmed yet."

Kay. Kimberly thought about the time they had met that first day she came to the White House.

"I met her once. She's a doll isn't she?"

"You bet she is. Everybody and his brother are lusting after her at the House." Larry laughed, watching his wife's face widen with curiosity.

"Not you, I hope."

"Not to worry." He crushed a big yawn.

"That's all?"

94

"Yep. That's all the women we've got."

Could it be Kay? No. She was too much like Millicent. Too ambitious. Stone needed a real woman. Someone he could have fun with. Someone who could give him a good time. And she had that scar. No, it wasn't Kay.

Kimberly went down to the dining room and poured herself a vodka martini, with an olive as big as the diamond hanging from her neck. She felt restless and impatient. No Valium before bedtime, the doctor had said, again. The diet pills were taking effect; she had not touched food all day and she felt lighter already. Her man would like that.

Maybe she had been wrong about him. Maybe he was just overworked. She mustn't forget, he was the President of the United States. She chased down a Halcion with vodka and wandered into the darkened living room. She turned on the TV.

The 11 o'clock news opened with Kay Kemeny and Bob Stone.

"President Stone will be visiting East Hampton for an annual softball game to raise money for the arts. Joining the President at bat will be Catherine Kemeny."

Kimberly's heart raced and she began gasping for breath.

She clicked off the remote, but the ghostly imprint of her lover's face remained.

"Angel," she murmured to the fading image, tears springing to her eyes. "Please angel, please don't leave me."

* * *

Wiesbaden, Germany

Martin Bauermann flicked off the audio cassette player and sat back in his chair. He listened to the Americans for the tenth time, and still could not find the answer to one question. How would the chips fall if the Americans prosecuted Vorody?

"They'll have to find him first," Heinrich Dorff said when he heard the news at head office in Stuttgart. "And when they do, we'll get to him before them."

That's what worried Bauermann.

Not that he didn't think the head of The Fifth had what it took to destroy Vorody once he found him. But he wasn't sure the gamble of giving leads to the woman was the best insurance money could buy.

"We're everywhere, Martin. Once she locates him, he can't escape us," Dorff said after he sent her the E-mail.

Sooner or later someone would get to Vorody. And then he would trade everything he held back about KGB and Stasi positions in the West in exchange for his life.

Bauermann turned to the window and scrutinized the horizon. Most of what he saw belonged to his organization. The Fifth, KGB and Stasi agents like himself, had "escaped" from the wrong side of the Wall in the 60's and 70's and acted as very efficient implants in the West. They had spent time studying Western ways and mastering their skills. One by one, they found executive employment in powerful West German firms where they functioned magnificently, all the while gathering information for Stasi.

When the Iron Curtain fell and East Germany dissolved, their operations were dismantled. The People raided Stasi's files. No one knew, certainly not Martin Bauermann, how much those files revealed. Those at the highest echelons in East German Intelligence anticipated a bleak future. Some, like Markus Wolf and his chief lieutenants, were too prominent not to prosecute. But those who were well undercover in Western Europe and America were told by Heinrich Dorff to continue operating as before.

They became mercenaries for hire and business boomed.

An Iranian group wanted to buy weapons, who better to broker the deal than the same Stasi agents who serviced them over the years? Iraq had to replace nuclear components right under the noses of the Americans. Who better to assemble them from dozens of separate purchases by dozens of legitimate companies. Libya needed a chemical warfare factory smuggled in part by part. They couldn't very well call Federal Express. Instead, they called Heinrich Dorff.

Because they had extraordinary skills and training, The Fifth could accumulate vast profits, which were piling high, among other places, in Bauermann's coffers. Their power was greater than any other crime organization. The world was their apple.

But there was a man in America who could put them all behind bars.

There were no options here. The Fifth had to be the first to find Vorody.

* * *

Berlin, Germany

Shimon's snitch stuck out from behind the bar at the Viking's Cave like a fixture, along with the paraffin stove and the damp wooden counter, where roaches strolled among dirty beer mugs, undisturbed. The five foot hunting scene above was covered by huge brown patches of cooking grease and mold.

It was past closing time, but Jack the bartender rose high on this toes to greet them.

"Shimon told me you'd be coming."

Jack came out from behind the bar. He was about 5 foot 2, not a dwarf technically, but a short man if there's ever been one. Stevie tried to contain his shock.

"I think you know what we need," he said, checking his back.

Jacobi was busy closing the door behind the last customer who seemed too drunk to relinquish the wooden pillar near the toilet.

Stevie placed a well used bill, 500 marks, into the miniature hand.

"Tell me."

"The Fifth put out the word several years ago about Vorody. Anyone who brings him to them gets rich. Anyone who holds back is dead."

"And?"

"That's all I know."

Stevie turned to look at Jacobi.

"It's all he knows?" he asked.

Jacobi gave him a nod.

In a sweep, Stevie grabbed the midget's neck, holding his Adam's apple between his fingers. With the other hand he locked his short arm and twisted it up his back, lifting the man by arm and neck high above the bar. Jack's face turned crimson and his body jerked, his mouth gasping for air. His shoulders started to shake.

"Enough," Jacobi said. "Don't kill him."

Stevie dropped the small man at his feet.

"So. Are you sure that's all you know?"

Jack's eyes rolled in his head and stopped at the door.

"Locked," said Jacobi, dangling the key in front of him.

From the unlit street came the wailing sound of a siren.

"Talk," Stevie ordered. "Who's protecting him?"

Jack swallowed.

"CIA. Someone in Wiesbaden prepared his papers and sent him to America."

"Who?"

"If I knew, I wouldn't be around to tell."

* * *

Langley, Virginia

Gene Boren stared at the three codes blinking on the screen. He smiled. Orwell, his computer, never disappointed him. He pushed "Enter" and the codes cleared. Three names appeared, indicating who had accessed the Kemeny file before him: Stafford Greenhill, Wade Jennings and Tim Bartlett.

Stafford Greenhill was easy to figure. He was CIA's Mortician. His job was to bury investigations at Justice. Wade Jennings was in charge of the Kemeny termination. But who was Tim Bartlett?

The name didn't ring a bell.

He called a friend in Operations and asked the right questions.

The answer came in a little over three hours. Bartlett was a Cowboy, and he worked from within the Agency for Edwin Racklee.

Right now, he was stationed in Wiesbaden.

* * *

Frankfurt, Germany

"I'm going to Paris tomorrow. Don't make a move," Jacobi announced on the fifth day.

"What the hell am I doing here then?" asked Stevie, barely containing his anger. "All we've learned is that Vorody's got protection."

"Peter and Hans will be in touch. Trust me."

"What if they're not?"

"You don't know these two.

"Here's a number where you can reach me in two days. And Stevie. Wait for me."

THIRTEEN

She was rehearsing the Education Fund address, her rounded, purposely sluggish vowels projecting outward with intended elegance, when Clancy Leduc burst in.

"Millie, I'm so sorry. I wanted to wait but then I thought I'd catch you before you left for San Francisco and —"

"Get to the point."

Leduc's copious lips folded at the corners in an expression of pain.

"Oh Clancy," the First Lady came around the desk and took his hand in hers. "Talk to me."

"It's about this Grigor Vorody business." Leduc squeezed her hand as he spoke. "Kemeny is becoming a threat."

"Oh?"

"Yes." He inched closer. His eyes, beady and permanently feverish, devoured her face, and his breath, a bit off, tickled her nostrils.

"I have reason to believe that he's linked to some of the former CIA. They don't want him prosecuted."

Millicent pulled away.

"Gordon's CIA."

Leduc followed her behind the desk.

"Millie, they're still operating, off the books — and we need them. And the timing is wrong. If she gets him, it'll take a good four years to go to trial. Until then, they'll trash this administration. That takes care of Bob's next term and kills our plans for you. If you're going to run when Bob's done, you can't afford to have him tangled in a CIA scandal."

"How do we stop it?"

"Only Bob can."

* * *

Paris, France

The bar in the hotel Villa Sud on Boulevard Haussman was a classic relic, modernized just enough to suit the third class business traveler.

Jacobi met Antoine at a table facing the entrance at exactly 6 pm the day he arrived. In the sunny lobby, clearly in view from where Antoine sat nursing a tall drink, his men read newspapers patiently, like transients killing time. Jacobi knew he could speak freely here. Antoine owned the place.

Jacobi and Antoine were close. Their fathers did business in the fifties, and Antoine's Papa never could understand why Ezra didn't join them. He would have been a rich man by now. And he wouldn't have to put up with all the politics. But Antoine was secretly happy for his friend. Ezra had his freedom.

Antoine was in his late 40's, older than Ezra by a few years, but he seemed younger. His rosy face was framed by unruly ash blond hair and he wore black horn-rimmed student glasses, which always fell low on his nose. There was something familiar about him, as if you'd seen him somewhere before, yet he didn't look like anyone in particular. He had a charming accent and a tendency to speak French and English at the same time.

"Sorry I couldn't meet you earlier," Antoine said after they settled in. "It wasn't easy to find what you desired. Ever since Union Sovietique fell, it's still not easy. *Plus ça change plus c'est la même chose.*"

"It sure is. Things don't change in America either. Only there they don't believe me when I tell them." Jacobi sounded bitter for a moment. "But it's getting better, you'll see."

"When? Je doute. The former KGBs are everyplace. You know what The Fifth is doing here in Europe."

"Who doesn't?"

"Your man, Vorody — he's le top in the profession, tu comprends? The best thing coming from America."

"From America?" Jacobi said dismayed. "You mean from Russia?"

"Mais non, mon petit frere. America. Vorody was CIA from the start."

"No, you got that wrong. He became CIA later. Then he defected to the States. I got that from Wiesbaden. CIA top people told me."

"Naive, mon ami. Very naive. You must never repeat what I'm telling you now. Or you're dead. Listen.

"Vorody was CIA since he was a child. His father, Sandor Vorody, disappointed by the communists, gave the CIA his son. Grigor was 15 when they took him to Camp Peary. Pavlov knows now. KGB knows. Even Stasi knows. He became KGB after he was trained by CIA for 10 years. He studied in Moscow, at KGB Academy. He was the perfect implant. He played the game for Pavlov and CIA made sure the KGB believed him.

Pavlov then asked Vorody to go to CIA and become a double agent. Can you imagine the irony? Why not? Pavlov liked him, he spoke American like a real American, and he could be trusted. He was the son of a communist hero. He became CIA the second time. So he was a triple agent most of his life. The only one I know who remained alive. Brilliance. Genial! The pride and gloire of the Americans. Caused KGB to fall apart much faster than it would have. They were destroyed by him in every way. Le moral. Terrible blow."

Jacobi couldn't believe his ears. This was right up there with Kim Philby! Genius standing alone.

"I can't believe the Americans were capable of that," he murmured.

Antoine started to laugh. "I know. After all your theory about how they have thick heads with human intelligence. This was all human, no computer, and it lasted a quarter of a century!"

Jacobi thought of Stevie, whom he had teased about this in Frankfurt, and felt like calling him tonight. But he couldn't tell him about Antoine. And it was too dangerous for him to know what he'd just found out.

"Mon frere," Antoine interrupted his reverie, "don't worry. The men who made this Vorody implant are no longer with CIA. They are the old OSS masters and their students. Their main man is Racklee. He ran this all alone, hidden from the management. He took it with him when those idiots threw him out."

So Racklee won the war for them. Incredible.

"Now," Antoine continued, "you can see why the American public can never find out about Vorody. They had to do a lot of horreurs to bring him up in position at KGB. Betrayal of American lives. Dirty work. Filthy. But it was worth it for them. It's done everywhere, only the Americans did it better, and for a very long time."

"It can't come out." Jacobi mused to himself, weighing the consequences for Kemeny's confirmation. She was in big, serious, deadly trouble. They would do anything to stop her from exposing Vorody.

So they should. What the hell was she trying to prove anyway. She should have figured out something wasn't kosher by now.

"They brought Vorody into the States," Antoine continued. "The Former CIA, those who call themselves Cowboys, have him hidden somewhere. Where you my brother should NOT find him. Don't even try. You are as good as dead if you do."

Jacobi had 20 years experience with Antoine and his Papa. They were never wrong. They had their people always watching every point on the European map. They ran safe houses, arms and vehicle supplies, escape routes, all that at high prices for the terrorists and their hunters. They had eyes and ears inside every intelligence agency. If they said Vorody had been CIA from the start and CIA boosted him sacrificing their own, and if Kemeny got the proof, then his dossier would rip the CIA to shreds, publicly. The public outcry would force Congress and the President to purge the CIA. The Cowboys would be first to go.

Sweet revenge. He could destroy them just like they tried to destroy him. But who was he to take them on? A fly on the wall of intelligence. A small, independent ex-Mossad who had fallen in disgrace.

"Antoine, I'm taking your advice, don't get me wrong. I will not get involved. But give me something to take back. Proof that Vorody is in the United States.

Passport and photo. That's all. This way Stevie's prosecutor friend can get confirmed because she has proof that he was allowed into the country. And then no one finds anything more because I don't tell the rest of the story."

"You'd be crazy if you did. You'd be dead and buried and I'd be responsible. What's more, anyone who could mastermind Vorody could also put two and two together and know Papa and I told you."

"You know you can trust me."

"Good. Go to Londres tonight. Wait for me there. It may take a couple of days. I know exactly where to get what you need. It's with Vorody's biggest enemies. I'll find some way to bring them to you. But you must promise me one thing. If they ask you to find him, play along until you get the documents. Then don't do a damn thing about it. Not a thing. They tried everything to find this man. They will not be surprised if you don't succeed."

* * *

Langley, Virginia

It was already 4 am.

Gene Boren stared blankly at the transcript. It was the last of Kemeny's court cases. He had only four hours left to find her Achilles heel. For a moment he wondered if she had one, but he caught himself. They always did.

This one was a civil case against a former Ethiopian torturer living in Atlanta. Ngobi Shururu, political refugee residing in the U.S., had been called by Kemeny to testify against him.

He read the part where the defense lawyer asked about Shururu's whereabouts before the trial. She had just come in from Paris with her sister, who was also scheduled to testify.

"And how did you enter the U.S.?"

"Through the Visitor's Line at JFK."

"And your sister?"

"The same."

"Did your sister have a visa?"

"Ms. Kemeny wrote a letter to ask for visa for trial, Sir."

"So your sister was returning to Paris after the trial?"

"No. She was going to live with me, Sir. I found her a job cleaning hotel."

"Where"?

"In New York City."

In New York City, Boren repeated to himself.

"Did Ms. Kemeny make you any promises in exchange for your testimony?"

"No, Sir. But she said she help us get green card for my sister."

Boren smiled. Finally, this was it. Everyone in that courtroom had missed it.

102

Kemeny knew about the sister's intention to live in the U.S. And yet she wrote an official letter indicating only a temporary visit to testify.

Beautiful! Catherine Kemeny, nominee for the Deputy Attorney General for Human Rights, had conspired with the Shururu sisters to deceive and defraud the U.S. government.

He had a felony.

* * *

He sat around his room at the Frankfurter Hof Saturday and Sunday, counting the bleak hours before Monday. He ate too much and started to smoke again.

He was watching CNN's headline news for the twenty-fourth time Saturday night when Kay called.

"I'm going on Sally Carmen next week, and I have to release something new."

"All I know is that he's in the United States. But I have promises from two sources."

"Who?"

"They're reliable. I met them with Jacobi."

"Are you sure about Jacobi?"

He didn't answer.

"When did they say they'd come through?"

"They didn't. Kay, you know this business. It can take time."

He hung up after promising her he'd try something else. No later, she implored him, than Monday.

But what? He couldn't very well gather intelligence from a hotel room in a city he'd never seen before and a language that was a total mystery. Even if he decided not to listen to Jacobi, he had no place to go.

FOURTEEN

Miami Beach, Florida

Edwin Forest Racklee spent the day poring over the thick file Jennings had compiled on Kay Kemeny. He studied the Shururu case and Boren's proposal. It was smart. But it wasn't a sure bet. And Racklee believed in certainty.

He rose and entered his communication bubble, dialing eleven digits and waiting exactly five seconds. When the signal came, he spoke.
"I want 24 hours surveillance on Catherine Kemeny."

* * *

East Hampton, New York

Just as dawn started to break, the President kissed the soft skin above Kay's breast.
"I've got to go, my love," he whispered. "I'm sorry."
He asked Roger and the others to stay behind and walked alone on the beach, slowly, noticing for the first time in years the beauty of the morning. It was past 6 and the sun had risen from the waves, still sleepy, wrapped in feathers of fog. The air was dewy and the spider web of moisture kept prisoner for a few more moments the first golden rays of the day.
He was in love with Kay, and that changed everything.
He wanted to keep her near him. He wanted to live up to her.
His life before he met her suddenly seemed unmemorable, unnecessary. How would he ever go back to things the way they used to be?

* * *

Miami Beach, Florida

Vorody contacted him exactly four days after they met at the Sandy Beach Motel.

A messenger delivered an envelope containing a photograph of a building like any other. One might think it was an apartment building except for a partial plaque: ... Home For Children. Even without the plaque Racklee knew the place well. He had studied every bit of Kemeny's file. But how did Vorody know?

He drove to Palm Beach in less than two hours.

The building was cobalt blue, with canary yellow window sills. But, on closer inspection, its artificial brightness was the only redeeming feature about the Drug Rehabilitation Home For Children. Decay transpired though fresh paint like an act of violence.

A maze of giant mangrove gathered around the front, their roots pushing deep against the walls on either side of the entrance arcade. A golden Moorish gate, battered by too many winds, led to the roped, empty pool: Closed for renovation. The smell of acid still lingered in the air. The workers must have just quit for the day. Who could blame them? Heat, at South Florida summer high, carried the acrid odor all the way to Racklee's car as he pulled in the deserted driveway.

So there it was. Mary Kemeny's workplace.

He got out reluctantly.

He walked through the back alley to the ocean side of the compound. It must be dead noon, he thought, noticing that the building cast no shadow on the beach. The eerie silence of the hour and the absence of shadow startled him, making him feel vulnerable. He came back the opposite way, treading carefully through trash cans, checking the grounds.

Vorody appeared from nowhere, looking composed, comfortable in a short sleeved Che Guevara jacket and khaki pants of heavy twill.

"It's good she retired to Florida, Lieutenant, or else we'd have to travel far."

A single royal palm he hadn't noticed before stood, grand and uncluttered, in the middle of the short walkway to the beach. Beneath it, a single white wicker table with two chairs.

They sat, and Racklee noticed behind it an expanse of tropical foliage filled with children's art.

There were wood and metal sculptures in the shape of elephants and starfish, white canvas stained with crayon scribbles and funny, naive drawn faces whose features matched the disorder of the trees.

Racklee waited in silence.

"They're away on a trip today. The place is empty."

He shrugged.

"I can see."

"You studied my memoirs?"

Racklee wiped his forehead with the back of his hand.

"I did."

"So tell me how you plan to stop Kemeny."

Racklee told him, in all detail, the story of Gene Boren's smear.

"But," he cautioned, "you know I never trusted Containment completely. That's why I've got my own plan. Don't worry."

"Lieutenant, I don't worry. That's why I wanted us to meet here."

A question marked rose between Racklee's brows.

But Vorody sat silent again, and Racklee grew restless. The heat had risen higher than before and choked him now, like cellophane. He was bagged in heat. His heart beat much faster than normal, and his pills were in the car. He started to rise.

"You would have liked her father. Nicholas Kemeny."

Grigor pinned him with his eyes.

"Lieutenant, you know I'll never ask you to do something against the national security."

"I do."

"Then you'll know this is a favor, to a friend."

Vorody paused.

"Try, if you can, not to hurt Catherine or Mary Kemeny."

* * *

Well well, Racklee thought, driving away on the scenic road he had taken so many times with Martha. Grigor was getting stupid in his old age. Not any less dangerous. Maybe more so, now that he let personal issues get in the way of damage control.

Protecting Catherine Kemeny was a new one. As if he didn't have enough restrictions placed on him already. First he had the President falling apart over Kemeny. The idiot. You'd think presidents could keep their dicks in their pants long enough to finish their terms.

Then he had the media and every bleeding heart in the universe crying out for Kemeny to be confirmed in that ridiculous job. Human Rights Chief.

And now, he had Vorody asking for personal favors. How on earth was he supposed to control this mess?

Vorody had clearly developed an emotional attachment to the family. He had him arrange green cards for them while he was still in Hungary. Later he got the daughter a scholarship.

The fool!

The coolness of his study came as a welcome surprise. Things were orderly, expected. The comfort of his tall leather chair and his first taste of bourbon soothed his mind. He swallowed two pills, and felt his pulse slow down. He rested in the undisturbed silence, contemplating Grigor's bizarre loyalty.

How could he promise to spare the girl, if Containment failed? Unless the President had the balls to get up sometime before those hearings and say the four magic words: "I withdraw Catherine Kemeny."

* * *

"Maybe you should withdraw her, Bob."

"Why, Mill? She's perfect!"

"Was. She was perfect."

"She's getting back on track. She'll feed the press more news on Vorody soon."

"Her news is bad news."

"Why?"

"It pits us against CIA. They won't let her prosecute Vorody. They'll smear her, make us look like fools, and you'll have to pick up the pieces."

"I can't believe this. Leduc got to you. The man is a maniac. I have all of this in control. All of it. Relax, will you, Millie?"

* * *

Frankfurt, Germany

Stevie left his hotel room Monday afternoon and, two hours later, pulled his rental car behind the gray apartment building in Wiesbaden. He found a used car lot and waited.

At 8 pm Peter and Hans walked out, accompanied by a third man. He watched them shake hands with the older man and leave. The man opened the door of a gray BMW and his face shone in Stevie's lights.

It was one of his instructors from 10 years back. Intelligence training!

Bartlett. Yes. Tim Bartlett.

He hadn't seen him since those days but he hadn't changed much — a lot grayer, but still lean, tall, straight as an arrow. Nobody liked him at Langley. They said he was a mean bastard. He only cared for the guys with balls. Bartlett would remember him.

He got into his car alone. Stevie gave him two blocks.

Two miles later, Bartlett pulled into a shopping center, parked in the crowded lot, and went into a fast food restaurant. Stevie waited ten minutes and followed him inside.

"Tim, Stevie Vitt," he said at the self-service counter. "We worked together 10 years ago."

Bartlett turned and looked at him with milky blue, dead eyes. He took his tray and sat at a table, motioning Stevie to join him.

"Remind me."

Dropping his voice, Stevie said, quickly, "Stevie Vitt, DEA. Intell training at Langley."

Bartlett nodded. The eyes stayed flat but the mouth smiled.

"So what brings you to Wiesbaden?"

The next morning Stevie awoke to the hush of an envelope being slipped under his door. When he went to look, the corridor was empty.

In the envelope, there were two photocopies. One was a USSR passport with the photo of a man in his forties, thick black-framed glasses and very flat black hair, the kind of hair you saw on the Chinese. The name on it was Grigor Vorody. The other was a U.S. passport of a naturalized citizen, a man about 50 to 55 with dark wavy hair and brown eyes. The name read Gregory Varda.

That was it! There was no other document, no file, no explanation. He put the papers away carefully in his attaché case.

Stevie was singing cheerfully in the shower when the phone rang.

"Recognize my voice?"

It was Bartlett.

"Yes Sir! Thank you!"

"Got something for you. Know the Bruder Cafe in Romenplatz?"

"I've been there."

"Good. Lunch at 14 hours."

Stevie arrived at the cafe a few minutes early and took a seat at the front, right on the sidewalk. He ordered a beer.

Had Jacobi been there, he would have known something was wrong about Bartlett's rendezvous.

Jacobi would have been alerted from the start by the late hour. At 2 o'clock the lunch crowd waned, leaving the cafe empty and the alleys full. Jacobi would have arrived early, checked both approaches to the restaurant and stood against the wall, observing.

After the clock struck 2, ten minutes passed, Jacobi would have been worried by Bartlett's delay. He would have scanned each passer-by, and looked beyond their faces in every direction. He would have seen a tall, broad shouldered man, much like Bartlett, about 100 yards to the left, leaning against a wall under a store awning, reading a tourist map. Keeping his eyes on him, Jacobi would have noticed two young Syrians in matching windbreakers and shoulder bags approach him, pretending to focus a camera in Stevie's direction. He would have understood then that he was hunted. He would have risen and run long before Bartlett disappeared from his view, before the Syrians started their final approach toward Stevie, before it was too late.

But Stevie did not notice the passing of time. He listened to the light music playing in the cafe's loud speakers and to the fragments of conversation. He was out of trouble at last. He was about to deliver Kay Kemeny her nomination. A smile still lit his handsome face when the Syrians moved toward the shop window just to the left, slid along the wall and entered the cafe. He did not hear them return through the center aisle behind his back, or reach deep into their shoulder bags, nor did he feel the shock of the bullets that entered his head through the left, ravaging his brain.

Stevie died thinking that Tim Bartlett could be trusted. Bartlett was CIA. He was American. He was a friend.

FIFTEEN

London, England

Ezra Jacobi stepped out of the elevator at his Grosvenor Square hotel and followed Antoine's man to the men's room. He got his instructions, washed his hands and walked out undisturbed.

He walked right past two British MIV's and into the street where two unmarked cars waited on both sides of traffic, just like they had two hours ago at Heathrow. He turned right, and right again, onto a narrow street, half-blocked by a delivery truck. One MI5 was tailing him. The two cars followed.

He quickened his step.

He was about to pass the double-parked truck when it started moving forward. It pushed back and forth going over the sidewalk, as if the driver was trying to make a U turn. Jacobi squeezed past on the sidewalk, leaving the two MI5's hopelessly trapped.

On the other side of the truck the road was clear, except for a parked black van with its passenger door wide open.

"Jump in," a voice ordered.

Fifteen minutes later they dropped Jacobi off in front of a nondescript restaurant in a neighborhood he did not know. A leather-clad maitre d' greeted him in French, and led him to a plush private room. On his way past the bar Jacobi noticed a few of Antoine's men. The restaurant was theirs for the night.

He found Antoine sitting alone at a table set for three. He rose with difficulty from the overstuffed red velvet banquette.

"Our guest sent a message that he'll be a little late."

They chatted, but then fell silent, listening to the muted sounds coming from the restaurant.

Thirty minutes later the maitre d' ushered in the third man.

Jacobi's heart began to race as the gray, tired face moved closer. He wasn't yet one hundred percent sure but the man who just entered the airless room looked an awful lot like —

"Heinrich Dorff. Pleasure to meet you Herr Jacobi."

The head of The Fifth! If he told anyone he was sitting with Dorff, they wouldn't believe him.

"We have what you need," Dorff said, looking straight at him.

He took out an envelope and placed it on the table.

"You have in here passport photos, before and after the physical change. New name. Last three addresses in the United States."

Jacobi stared at the sealed envelope, without touching it.

"And," he cleared his voice, "what can I do to repay your kindness?"

"We want Vorody."

He took from his breast pocket a packet of Black Russians and offered one to Jacobi.

"Thank you. I don't smoke."

Dorff tried without success to light the gold tipped cigarette.

"Five years we've been looking for him," he said, dropping the lighter on the table. It fell with a thud.

"Everyone who tries to find Vorody gets taken care of by Edwin Racklee." Antoine intervened. "He is dangerous."

"You should know how dangerous." Dorff leaned back in the velvet banquette. "You were in Frankfurt and Wiesbaden, weren't you, helping your friend Stevie Vitt."

How the hell did he know?

Jacobi took the lighter and shook it. It must have been some wartime souvenir. A small explosion ignited it after a few tries. Dorff bent forward and lit his cigarette slowly, until the black tip turned to ash.

He blew the smoke away from the table.

"They took Vitt down today at the Bruder Cafe."

Jacobi dug his fingers deeply in the silver lighter. It made a hissing noise, releasing a pool of smelly petroleum fluid that stained the table cloth, seeping through the eyelet pattern onto a patch of reddish wood. Surely he was wrong. He had warned Stevie not to leave the Frankfurter Hof. Damn, damn, damn! They killed Stevie!

Somehow, he managed to hold Dorff's stare. He was grateful for the silence. Dorff smoked. Antoine drank.

"I'm sorry," Dorff said at last. "I wasn't sure if you knew. That's why I was detained. I was getting the full report. Bartlett set it up. He used two Syrians — we know who they are. They took him out with two bullets in the head."

Jacobi dropped the lighter on the table, and looked away.

"He didn't suffer. It was quick. They planted heroin in his room at the hotel. 'Corrupt drug agent killed in drug deal.' Well, you know the drill."

He glanced at Antoine.

"You have a good opportunity to find Vorody, Herr Jacobi. Through your friend, Ms. Kemeny."

Jacobi unclenched his fist.

"She's not my friend."

"But she will be. You must understand that we want him dead long before she exposes him. This is a man who can tell too many stories."

So that was that, Jacobi thought sadly on his way to the airport the next morning. Antoine had said good-bye in the street reminding him not to do anything about Vorody. Give the woman the files and get the hell out. She's doomed, just like Vitt. When she gets close to catching Vorody, let Dorff know via Antoine and Papa.

Ezra Jacobi would have gladly stabbed Bartlett in the heart. He hadn't killed a man in fifteen years and even then he hated it. But Stevie's death weighed heavily on him.

He looked at his watch. In a few hours Eva would wake Aaron and Becky back in New York, and prepare their breakfast. They'd be warm and rosy from the heat in their room where their beds were stacked, Aaron on top, with a yellow plastic machine gun under his pillow, and Becky below. They'd walk out the door all crisp and clean and dressed in their school navies, asking when daddy was coming back, and Eva would say soon, honey, soon, and she'd bend halfway out the window to watch them get on the school bus.

Get the hell out, was Antoine's advice. Get the hell out of this mess, before they put a mirror before your mouth and slide you in a refrigerator drawer next to Stevie.

Dammit. He was right.

* * *

Wiesbaden, Germany

That night in Wiesbaden Peter and Hans paid for Stevie's mistake with their careers.

Hans met the end of his dreams in the familiar parking lot. He was exhausted but feeling good. He had succeeded in getting the passport copies to Stevie Vitt and had slid them under his door before he woke up that morning.

He was getting into his car when three Bundeskriminalamt officers approached with guns drawn. They ordered him up against the car roof, frisked him, checked his car and then his trunk. There, hidden beneath a blanket Hans had never seen before, was a kilo of hash and four Uzis. He was immediately handcuffed and placed under arrest.

Peter didn't even have a chance to leave his office. As he was making a last minute call, he received an impromptu visit from Internal Security. He was recalled immediately to the United States on a serious charge.

* * *

"This is it, Ed. I'm going on Sally Carmen."

"Kay, slow down. Please. Let's talk things over."

"I'm going, Ed, I'm taking these passport photos and this damned American name, Gregory Varda. I'm exposing that bastard on national television and I'm not letting anyone stand in my way."

"You can't just go."

"Why the hell not?"

Ed's voice came out with difficulty, choked with emotion. He had to say it, at the risk of frightening her.

"Because I just don't want to lose another friend."

Kay shook her head violently and started to cry.

Ed took her in his arms.

"My God, Kay," he murmured, "look what we've done to Stevie."

Ezra Jacobi felt like a spectator, watching the two friends mourn. He was the messenger who brought them Vorody's passport and Stevie's death. Maybe it was his fault too. He never told them about how Stevie helped him, nor about the guilt he felt for not being able to punish his killers. It was none of their business anyway. Let them keep dreaming that they could change the world. In the meantime the world was still a disgusting place.

They didn't know that Bartlett could have let Stevie live. He was no danger to anyone. He could have just let him be. Or pushed him down the wrong alley, given him a flawed lead, played with him and let him get back to Kemeny thinking he had found something great. Could Bartlett have known he had the photo and passport from Hans? Even if he did, all he had to do was take them away.

But Stevie had seen the photos. The documents. The name Gregory Varda. Stevie had a chance to take a look at the face Vorody had shown no one. Could he have saved Stevie, had he stayed in Frankfurt? Or would he be dead now too?

Enough already! He had to stop or he'd go mad with frustration.

He got up to leave.

Kay opened her eyes, swollen and red, and rushed to the door.

"Don't leave us, Ezra. We need you."

"No you don't," he answered uneasily. "You know everything I know. I left Stevie before he was shot. I read about it on the plane."

"You must tell me more," she implored him, blocking the doorway, taking his hands in hers. "You can't just leave us now. We know he was killed by the KGB."

Jacobi looked at her for the first time.

"Do we?"

Nothing had prepared Kay for his visit, so she was still in her filmy summer dress, barefoot, and with her hair clipped in a pony tail, like a school girl. Not what he had expected from the future Human Rights Chief. She was lovely. The kind of lovely that made Jacobi feel inappropriate even at the best of times, let alone today, in his rumpled army fatigue shirt, sweaty and dirty from the long trip back. Look at her. The beautiful shiksa of his dreams. He was tired and angry. He shouldn't have come.

He started for the door again. Kay grabbed his arm with a strength that surprised him.

What a woman, Jacobi caught himself thinking as she shook him hard, begging.

"Ezra, I need you. You're the only link I've got to Stevie's killers. Can't you see they're trying to keep me away from Vorody?"

The mention of that name reminded Jacobi to get out. The room suddenly felt like a prison, and Kay, this beautiful woman with those burning hands was the devil's temptation, put in his way to finally make him pay for his sins. To lure him into being a hero one last time. But she was right, damn her, she was right that they needed him. Look at her. She knew nothing about what was going on.

Was it guilt that tormented him, guilt at the thought that if he didn't help her she'd be killed? Guilt because he had just given her the Inquisitor's real face? Or was it that she made him dizzy with those almond-shaped eyes the color of honey, that lean tanned body naked under a thin layer of silk?

Jacobi shook her off. He didn't need to complicate his life with some beauty whose days were numbered.

"For the last time, Ms. Kemeny. I'm just a messenger. You're right. He was probably killed by the KGB."

"Where did you get the passport photos? Tell me."

"Stevie got them. He sent them to me. It was all Stevie."

Kay broke down again, and Jacobi couldn't help letting her lean on his shoulder. Nothing was going smoothly ever since he had come up against this Vorody business. Especially not the fact that at that very moment he was clutching Cowboy Enemy Number One. Talk about courting danger. He was out of his mind.

He slowly coaxed her away, but the devil had her hair caught in the button of his shirt collar. He couldn't help feeling her heartbeat and the heat of her breasts against his chest as he struggled to break free.

"At least let me give your name to Tommy O'Hara." Endicott said at last. "Stevie's boyfriend — he's FBI. He needs to hear this from you. Would you, please?"

Against his better judgment, Jacobi agreed.

* * *

"That was fantastic, Kay! Fifty million people watching, and Sally Carmen was incredible! Can't imagine what more they could want."

"So I take it you're pleased, Mr. President?" she said softly into the phone.

"I sure am. And, Kay, remember, right now everyone is on your side."

Leduc was uneasy, still concerned this might be a trap, a catch, something awful waiting to destroy them. Even Millicent started hinting that the Vorody angle was dangerous. To her it reeked of CIA. No wonder these two got along so well. They were both paranoid.

It was almost midnight and he was alone in The Library.

Roger came back with two double burgers and stone devoured them, thinking about Kay. This was the first time they had not seen each other for a full 24 hours.

He couldn't blame her for wanting to get away to Palm Beach for the weekend, away from this pressure, maybe even from him

Secretly, he wished her luck finding Vorody, even if his wife and Leduc were right and the CIA was involved. Fuck the CIA. They played games behind every president's back. The whole thing, if it happened, was Gordon's mess. It was Gordon's America that gave this murderer a U.S. passport and citizenship. It was Gordon's America that played the deadly game. Let Gordon and his Republicans take the heat.

Midnight rang differently somehow, now that it didn't announce Kay's arrival. A joyless sound, indicating only that it was time for a lonely and wakeful sleep.

He missed her voice, the heat of her body. Their long talks. He picked up the phone and started to dial her number again, but hung up as it began to ring.

Suddenly, the prospect of two days without her was dismal, magnified by the restless night ahead. He pictured tomorrow crawling by in Millie's company. How could he expect to return to his life without Kay when the time came?

He dozed at last on the bed where they had made love only yesterday.

He woke up the next morning in The Library, and realized he had slept there all night. That was against the rules. It was a little before 5 and the sun rose quickly before him, first a patch of deep burgundy, than mauve, then a wide smile of grapefruit pink. By the time it was all up there, a cheery yellow globe of a perfect August day, Bob Stone had already asked Roger to arrange for his plane.

* * *

There was always room at The Breakers for presidents and their entourage, especially now, after the last rush of seasonal tourists. Other hotels closed down in August, when the devastating heat blazed. Not the Breakers. The Breakers always kept a wing open for its regular patrons.

Stone's arrival in a black van with only six secret service guards went unnoticed on that understaffed, lazy Saturday afternoon. He went straight to his suite.

He dropped his overnight bag on the floor and, without stopping to admire the voluptuous decor, rushed to the South terrace. He could see the Rehab building, just a few hundred feet away, brightly set against the turquoise sea. He shielded his eyes with his hands. Was that her, the milky silhouette in the thick shade of a royal palm tree? She was close and yet impossible to distinguish. Heat distorted her body, dissolving her into the pastel sky.

He changed clothes impatiently, and started on the beach toward her. Three guards and Roger walked behind him and others were already stationed near the Rehabilitation Center, hidden from view.

He walked fast. From the cool hotel suite she had seemed reachable, a short walk away. But the heat took over, slowing his step.

She was leaning against the yellow backdrop of a beach chaise, cool in her white sarong, immersed in a thick book whose pages she turned slowly, looking up now and again at the ever shifting spots where the sun broke through the palm leaves.

He found a shaded place in the garden behind her and watched. The silence was raw and disconcerting, punctuated by the soothing break of small waves and the velvet hush of the garden alive with minute lizards, sleepy birds, tropical insects, year-round mosquitoes and musical trees.

"I'm so jealous of this peace," he said, his voice landing on the nape of her neck.

She quivered, but remained still.

"Why?"

"Because you chose it over me."

"I had to come," Stone explained at the hotel that evening, holding two tall flutes while Kay poured chilled white wine.

"I'm glad you did. I might have flown back today myself if you hadn't. Don't think it didn't cross my mind."

Stone started to pace the room, suddenly on edge.

"I think I'm in trouble with you, Kay."

She sighed. Bad news no doubt. She was grateful for the wine and the sun which had mellowed her almost beyond caring.

116

"I've always been in control of things —"

"Good for you, Stone," she said without irony. "I wish I could say the same."

"That's just it, Kay. I'm afraid this...you, you're changing that. I'm not so in control anymore. I depend on you, on being with you."

"Stone, you're breaking my heart," she smiled. "Now I see why presidents should all be married, old and dull. Anyway. I'm just a moment in your life."

He took her hand.

"I don't think so. I'd like to stay with you in this room for the rest of my life."

Kay smiled.

"It's either love, Mr. President, or you're getting all mushy as you age."

But his eyes stayed locked on hers, serious.

"What are we going to do, my love?"

SIXTEEN

"Honey buns!"

"Where are you honey buns?"

Devane gripped the receiver and started to count seconds on the grandfather clock.

"I said where are you sweetie. Don't you hear me anymore?"

He jumped. Kimberly was right beside him.

"For Chrissakes Kim! You almost gave me a heart attack."

"Who are you holding for?"

"Who else?"

"Where is he?"

"Florida. And I can't get anywhere near him on that stupid cellular phone."

"But it's August," Kimberly whispered.

"I know. Millicent's busy with single mothers and he wanted to get away."

"Awful man." Her lips moved, soundless. She was tired. It was only past noon. How many hours left until she could go to bed?

"Let me try this."

She took the phone. She dialed function, star, and a series of numbers, but the recording came back each time — "the cellular subscriber you are calling"—.

"I can't, Larry." A large tear fell down her cheek, and her voice faltered.

"I can't get him."

"Kimmie, what the hell...it's only a telephone! What's the matter with you lately? Relax, he must have turned it off. Maybe he doesn't want us to disturb him."

Kimberly's blood began to gather in her pale neck, staining it red.

"Why not?"

"Damned if I know. I heard he was meeting Kay Kemeny."

* * *

Six days after he ordered 24-hour surveillance on Kemeny, Edwin Racklee read the first report.

Kemeny stayed at the Regency Excelsior. Senator Endicott visited her daily. Each night at midnight she went to the White House, escorted both ways by Stone's personal guard.

She left D.C. just once, to go to New York. She took taxis, or was driven by friends. She did not use the White House car service.

She had breakfast in the hotel dining room. She was rarely alone.

Racklee swiveled in his chair toward the street, weighing his options. His house, neatly blocked from public view by a thick layer of palms, stood among the quiet subdivision like countless others in Miami Beach. No one could guess that its windows were bulletproof and that every entrance held a hidden trap. From the second floor where he had placed his study, Racklee could see the road in both directions and scan the view even further, around the block.

Murder of a public figure would bring too much heat.

Accidents? Too young for a heart attack or a fall in the tub. And suicide was out of the question. An automobile mishap on the other hand — well, even that was tricky with secret service so close behind.

At 6 pm, he turned on the evening news.

"Tragedy struck an innocent victim in Coral Gables in what has become an all too familiar pattern of urban violence."

He turned off the sound and let the words reverberate in his mind.

This was it. The perfect plan.

He stepped into his communications bubble and picked up the receiver.

"Give me Jennings."

He waited five seconds.

"I'm stocking a zoo. I need three black seals."

He hung up and dialed Wiesbaden.

"I need a reliable, long distance eye. One special problem." He listened for a while, his face impenetrable.

"No. Go to the Frenchman. Million tops. We take him in, he takes himself out. And get me two witnesses."

After he hung up, Racklee went to his window.

Everything around was orange, monotone, as if a child had painted the street with a giant crayon. The end of this day matched Racklee's solution. Up until now there was a rainbow of possibilities. Now, there was just one.

* * *

There was just one phone booth on the long arched toll bridge that linked Miami to Key Biscayne, and its location in the midst of a deserted automobile trail among endless miles of steel and cement made it an obvious target for vandalism. That day the phone hung useless, destitute, like an empty shell, when Grigor Vorody picked it up and tried his first coin.

The city lights flickered in the distance, muted by fog, like dying fireworks. This was the top of the bridge, the axis of the crossing. The point of no return.

He should have known.

Even before seeing them Grigor knew there were two men behind him. He heard their clunky weapons rub against thick leather, felt the thud of their studded boots on the burning asphalt, counted the two pairs of steps quickening toward him. It occurred to him that this might be the night. If Racklee sent them, it was now. If it was The Fifth he still had a chance.

He had often wondered how he'd feel when the moment came.

He turned sharply to face the two men, shocking them into a full stop. Relief enveloped him, strangely.

The men were young, black, and ready to trade his wallet for his life.

They tried.

Grigor rode his motorcycle back into Miami.

Nicholas's daughter had exposed his face to everyone and Racklee had allowed it. He had been betrayed.

The police could track him down and turn him into a circus beast. If they did, Racklee would ask him to make the supreme sacrifice. He'd say, stay with your role of KGB villain, plea bargain, and we'll make your life easier in jail. Let them throw stones at you. We'll get you good books, steak every day and a woman once a week. Minimum security.

"Well, Lieutenant," he murmured into his black helmet, "those days are gone. The American Century will have to dawn without me."

He found a working telephone booth in Black Grove.

He dialed the overseas operator and asked, collect, for a number in Switzerland.

There was a beep and he spoke close into the receiver.

"Code 15166685GLPOML."

He waited a long time until a man's voice came on the line.

"I want the contents transferred to Nassau."

He waited again, this time just a few seconds.

"Your password Sir, and speak up for the voice scanner to identify."

He spoke slowly Anton Pavlovitch Chekov's words:

"Greetings, last page of my life."

* * *

At 6:30 pm, Ezra Jacobi came out of his office building just across from Lincoln Center and started on his usual walk home. He enjoyed this routine, particularly in summer when Broadway was alive with people and a colorful string of outdoor cafes. Today, despite the hour, the evening still seemed far off. The sun shone behind him, red and fierce, strong enough to pierce through the heavy smog, aggravated by the relentless fumes and noises of rush hour.

Out of habit, he stopped in front of a restaurant window, checking to see if he carried any suitors in tow. He caught the reflection of a young man in a dark suit watching him from across the street. "I must have missed the others," he thought. They never sent just one man on surveillance. Unless the man was out there to hit.

He turned east toward Central Park.

The man kept behind him at 200 feet.

Jacobi advanced steadily, looking to the left and right.

He entered the park.

If it was a hit, this was the perfect place to strike.

He slowed his pace and slid his hand into his inside pocket. He took out a handkerchief, wiped his forehead and put it back, removing the small Beretta from his shoulder holster. He cocked it and tucked it in his belt.

The man followed closer behind.

Jacobi took a deep breath, and turned left into an underpass. He waited.

After a few minutes, he came out. The man was nowhere in sight.

He left the park and went into a small Irish pub.

He took his stool at the bar and ordered his usual. "Plus a light beer Mike, for a friend."

Minutes later a handsome man in his late twenties took the seat near him. Mike put a beer in front of the man. "It's from him," he said, pointing to Jacobi.

Jacobi took a good look at the man. Tall, muscular, naturally tan, with a short jet black crop and heart throb eyes. He looked like an actor. But his suit and shoes told Jacobi who he was. Their eyes met.

"Usually I get two Fibbies on my tail," Jacobi spoke first, "never just one. You guys don't trust one another to get it right." He paused, enjoying his surprise.

"What's on your mind?"

The man mimicked a salute.

"I'm looking for Stevie Vitt's contact from Frankfurt. I guess that's you," he said. His voice was at once strong and soft, a velvet baritone.

"That's right."

"I'm Tommy O'Hara. His roommate."

Good for you, thought Jacobi, circumspect. This guy was a fagellah?

"I'm sure you are, pal, but lately I'm not too friendly with the FBI."

"This has nothing to do with the Bureau. I'm on my own. I want to know who murdered Stevie."

"Who sent you?"

"Senator Endicott. The three of us were friends."

A few minutes passed. They each ordered another drink. Light beer again for O'Hara. They went to a table at the back.

"What do you make of the official story?" Jacobi broke the silence.

"Are you kidding me? I don't buy it."

"How about the KGB?"

"I don't buy that either. I know Ed and Kay do, but I don't. Why the hell would The Fifth bother with drugs and all that cover up. Bang, bang, that's that. It's how they operate. Hell, they'd want the whole world to know they get the job done. It's good publicity."

"Who then?"

Tommy looked around. He whispered reluctantly to Jacobi, "Cowboys, I think."

Smart kid. Smart and a looker. He could get all the shiksas lined up and pick who he wanted, Jacobi thought, sizing him up. God, why didn't you give it to me?

"Right."

"So what do they want with Vorody?"

"They have a huge stake in him. It goes back to the time he was in Russia. And to his disappearance. They don't want him to go public. They don't want him found. Kemeny would have gotten killed too if she hadn't exposed him on TV. Now she's got no more secrets."

He paused.

"But they'll try to get rid of her in other ways," Tommy said. "They won't let her get confirmed. They won't give her the government power to dig deeper."

Jacobi nodded.

"My bet is they'll discredit her. Any idea which department would handle it?"

"Clandestine Operations, no question."

"Any contacts there?" Jacobi asked, casually.

"One. But a good one."

"He won't talk."

"He might." Tommy beamed an enigmatic smile. His dark eyes turned to Jacobi, who turned beet red.

"By the way," Tommy continued, "did I tell you how grateful Kay and I are that you're helping us find Stevie's killers? I know now why he kept saying you were the greatest guy. Even after he was demoted." He reached for his hand.

Jacobi pulled away.

Why was it that everyone in this case had to be so nice, so beautiful and needy? Why was it he had to look like a jerk, like a heartless Jew if he told them all to leave him alone?

He sighed.

"Find out what you can about the smear. Let's see if we can mess up their plans."

* * *

New York JFK

The INS inspector looked past the nervous Egyptian woman onto the remaining line of visitors. Five minutes until quitting time and five customers left. All that because of a delayed flight from Brussels.

He pressed the button and waved the woman to the side.

Next was a guy in his 40's, olive skin, flat hair, bleary eyes, and a slight droop on the left side of his mouth. Typical business man in a rumpled suit.

Canadian passport, issued in Quebec, photo matched, lined up with the seal, round trip ticket for a full week.

Thirty five seconds later Racklee's Frenchman was admitted into the U.S.

* * *

"Oh thank you, Kimberly, thank you so much. This is... this is unexpected. It's a great surprise. Why, this is lovely. Thank you."

What else could he say?

She had shown up at the Oval Office unannounced and went right past Roger.

"Angel, you forgot our anniversary...Two years today! Your girl is here to remind you, you big bad man." She handed him a golden box. He opened it and found inside it two embroidered silk kimonos. One black and one pink.

"It's for the two of us."

She came behind him and bent forward, rubbing her face against his. "Come on Angel, take me to The Library."

He could smell peppermint and vodka on her breath. He shrugged her off.

"I'm sorry, honey. I've got at least another ten calls to make. I can't take any time today."

"Please, sweet, please, take an hour and let's just get away."

She lowered herself in his lap and her lips started to search for his. He tried to push her away.

"Kimmie, please stop. This is my office, remember? Someone could come in."

Direct One rang. He freed himself to pick up.

"Hello. Yes. Oh yes, Millie."

Kimberly looked away.

"Yes. No, I'm alone. Yes. The inauguration of the Womens' Wing is tonight? I can't believe they changed that. Too bad then. You know tonight I won't be able to attend. Yes. I'm glad you understand."

When he hung up, Kimberly turned back.

"Millie is gone for the night?"

"Yes. She's flying to New York with Leduc."

"So why can't I see you alone, angel, not even for a little bit?"

Tears were drowning her eyes again, ready to drop.

He packed the kimonos back into the box and put them in her hands.

"All right. Why don't you go first. I'll meet you there as soon as I'm done."

Two hours later he found her naked, half wrapped in the black kimono, lying on the undone bed in The Library.

"Kimberly —" he started, but she took his hands and covered them with kisses, shedding rivers of salty tears on his shirt cuffs.

"Why don't you ever want me anymore, angel? Tell me, what have I done?"

Her body started to shudder.

"Please, please don't leave me, angel, please don't leave me now, or I'll die, without you I'll die..."

He covered her with the blanket and held her against him until the tremors stopped.

"It's all right, sweetheart," he whispered, "it's all right."

She turned to him, her eyes lit up. She unbuttoned his shirt slowly and rubbed her cheek against his chest, licking his neck with her hot tongue, sneaking her hand down his belly to his zipper, taking him in her hands and rubbing him softly, kissing his mouth, guiding his hands to her breasts.

He obeyed her, wishing for a miracle.

He fondled her nipples as she slid down his body and started playing on him with her mouth. He tried to forget about everything, focusing his mind on the wet, delicious sensation.

But a moment later the image of Kay overcame him, and his body remembered.

Kimberly lifted her head from his lap. Her eyes died on his, like dimming light.

"I'm sorry Kim. This is not going to work. I'm seeing someone else."

Kimberly shook her head and looked right past him to the window. Outside it was magic hour. Five more minutes and the day would give in to night.

She rose silently and went, in a trance, to her handbag. She dug deep inside it and came out with a handful of pills and a silver flask. She swallowed the pills with vodka, gasping for air after each one.

Stone wanted to stop her at first but he thought better of it. Let her use them now, they'll help her calm down. She could start a detox program, he'd arrange it with Devane. But for now she needed all the help she could get.

"I'm so sorry, Kim. This is not something I planned."

She covered her breasts shyly, and grabbed her pink summer dress. The dress, flowered and cheerful, emphasized even more acutely her ravaged face. She dressed slowly, looking at Stone who still sat, fly opened, shirt unbuttoned, right there on the bed where they had made love so many times. When her hair was back in order, purse in hand, she went to him. She touched his forehead with her fingers, and brought her lips on his. He pulled back an inch. He saw his gesture mirrored in her face.

She went to the door and turned to him for the last time.

"I am so ugly. So old and fat," she murmured.

Then she was gone.

SEVENTEEN

The Queen's Regiment gathered at their summer house at sunset to spread Stevie's ashes into the sea.

Night fell quickly on the funeral, bright and fidgety. The moon was incandescent. Reflector-like stars burned circles of light in the pitch black sea.

Gene Boren saw Tommy O'Hara on the verandah, watching the darkness. He sighed. Not long ago, he had made a casual pass at Tommy and it had not been well received. He turned to face the room where couples still lingered, some on the Turkish sofas, some moving together in a slow dance. He sighed again.

A hand on his shoulder startled him — then his heart stopped.

"Tommy. I meant to tell you how sorry I am about Stevie."

He could lose himself in those eyes, he thought, looking at Tommy. He was so beautiful in his black linen shirt, open to his navel, his second-skin black jeans and his bare feet.

"How can I help?" he asked.

"Just be with me." Tommy's voice was smooth. Velvety. "Right now I need a friend, if I'm going to make it through these next few days. I've got to find out who's responsible for Stevie's death."

"Tell me about it. Maybe I can help."

Gene touched his hand.

"Well, you know the official version. Drug deal gone bad."

"I don't believe a word."

"Thank you."

The long, strong fingers curled against his.

"What was he doing in Frankfurt?"

"Helping Catherine Kemeny. She's trying to locate a former KGB. Stevie was tracking something over there. Obviously he got too close."

Gene thought back at the names who acccessed the file. Greenhill, Jennings, Bartlett. Wait a minute. Bartlett was stationed in Wiesbaden. Near Frankfurt.

This was not the sort of fire Tommy should play with.

"You're not alone," he said, taking both his hands.

Tommy's eyes shone with tears.

"It's good to hear you say that. I'm going to take a leave starting tomorrow. To find out who did this."

"Don't be a fool," Gene snapped. He pulled back. "This is the work of CIA contractors. Promise you'll stay away."

There it was. He had done it. He let out what he knew. His forehead grew damp. His hand was wet.

"I appreciate you're concern Gene. I do. But I can't take this lying down."

126

"Who are they? Do you at least know?"

Tommy pinned him down with his dark, angry eyes.

"Do you?"

He had to save Tommy from making a deadly mistake. Those eyes —. He caught his breath enough to say:

"I do." He looked away. "I also know they could kill you too."

Tommy pulled his hand from his.

"Do I look like a child to you?"

Yes you do, Gene thought. A beautiful, perfect, ideal child. A child I would do anything to hold and never let go. Tommy O'Hara, I would give you my life.

"I work for FBI remember?" Tommy continued, "I knew what I was in for. I've been ordered to look the other way more times than I can remember. But something's very wrong when they kill us for damage control."

"What are you going to do?"

"I haven't decided yet. I'll probably just go over there and take them out. Unless —"

"Unless?" Gene asked.

"Unless I can find a way to ensure Kemeny gets confirmed. That would be the best revenge. Whatever it is they're afraid of would come out. And they'd pay in spades for Stevie's death."

"That's dangerous too."

"Relax Gene, I know you work for them. It's OK. When they bury me you can let the public know I was corrupt too. Hell, it's your specialty. I'll be honored if they assign you to airbrush my life after I'm gone."

He turned away, but Gene Boren pulled him back, close to him, close enough to feel the heat of his chest against his.

"No Tommy, you've got it all wrong. It's not what I'm about. I'm not like them. I want you to live. I want you to be with me."

Tommy did not move. Only his eyes caressed him, long before he spoke.

"I want that too."

* * *

Ali Murani was happy with his new job as night manager at Gotham Mini-Storage on West 47th Street, near the piers of the Hudson River. He had paid $4,500 for his green card, social security card and driver's license. Not a bad package deal when you consider how impossible it was to get the real thing.

Ali liked America and he certainly liked his job. Apart from occasional paperwork, he was a glorified security guard. That was especially good, since he needed to catch up on his sleep before starting his day job, driving a cab.

That night Ali was awakened by a dark haired man, droopy mouth, dressed in a sweatshirt, jeans and Reeboks.

He waved hello, went straight to the slot and inserted his pass card. Just another customer. Ali went back to sleep.

The man reached the fourth floor and walked, cautiously, along every aisle. When he was sure he was alone, he went to the fourth row and opened a locker.

He pulled out one large suitcase. In it was a mirror, a custom case, a scope, several shells, and a rifle, disassembled and packed neatly to fit. And a 9 mm Glock semi-automatic pistol with a silencer.

He carefully inspected every piece of equipment. No numbers. Untraceable. Safe. Finally, the American passport, taped at the bottom of the case.

It was all as ordered. By Tim Bartlett for Edwin Forest Racklee.

* * *

"Bob, sorry to call you so late. Did I wake you?"

"No, no Larry, I was reading tomorrow's address. What's going on?"

It was 2 in the morning and it wasn't like Larry to call. Did Kimberly tell him anything?

"I... I don't even know how to tell you, Bob. I'm so profoundly embarrassed. I'm afraid I've put our entire Administration to shame.

"Larry, what are you talking about?"

"It's Kimberly."

"Talk to me."

"She took more than a hundred sedatives. I found her in her bedroom. Bottles of pills. Empty bottles everywhere."

Stone's heart raced. Kimberly was dead? A throbbing pain flashed behind his forehead. Was this what it was like to have a stroke? He made a mental note to have a check up the next day.

Kimberly was dead, and it was his fault. He was silent.

"She's been taking them for a long time, Bob."

He remembered the last time they were together. Kimberly's cumbersome passion was finally at rest. God, how he hated himself for that thought.

"Larry, I...I don't know what I can say. I'm sorry. What can I do to help?"

"Thanks Bob."

"Larry, I hate to bring this up so soon, but you know how it is, anything we can do to, well, to keep this under wraps with the press? After all you don't want Kimmie to be remembered as an unstable...well. Suicide."

"No, hey, Bob, no, you misunderstood. She'll be all right."

"What?"

"She pulled through. She's sleeping now. It was touch and go right after they pumped her stomach, but she'll be fine. I found her. I found her just in time."

Stone was mute.

Thank goodness. She was alive.
Now he had every reason in the world not to see her anymore. She embarrassed them all.

"Larry, you must promise me you'll give her my very best wishes for a speedy recovery. She'll understand of course that we must not see her at the White House until she is completely cured."
"Yes, Bob, of course. She had a manic depressive phase, that's all. A lot of women will relate. Trouble sleeping, diet pills, you know. And one night she had a drink. An allergic reaction with alcohol.
She's going to a therapy clinic in the Rockies, in Canada, to dry out. Lake Louise. Far enough to keep the press away."
After they hung up, Larry Devane looked at his sleeping wife. With all those tubes in her and no make up, in that faded blue hospital gown, she seemed so innocent, so vulnerable. And so slight.

* * *

"Ms. Kemeny, is it fair to say that you came to the President's attention because of your successful convictions in a number of human rights cases?"
"Mr. Folsom, perhaps you should ask him."
Mike Folsom smiled and sat back on the wing chair he had strategically positioned before a stately vase of orchids, the perfect frame to his face, marked by the creases of age and the heavy makeup. The camera was pointing directly at Kay, ready to take the classic sweaty upper lip close-up that had made "Friday Night" a hit for over 25 years.
Kay knew that a tough question would come, as did the rest of America. Folsom was reliable that way. Every time he leaned backwards, he thought he tricked his "victims" into believing they too could relax. And then he popped a show stopper.
"Did you ever break the rules, Ms. Kemeny? Did you ever do anything illegal?"

This was the stage where Folsom liked to remain polite.
Kay leaned back on the tan velvet couch that matched her skin tone and illuminated her eyes. Ed Endicott's choice.
"No." she replied.

"You have never been tempted, not even once?"

Kay inched closer to Folsom, forcing a two-shot.

"Tempted?" she said, with a hint of sarcasm. "Tempted, yes. Succumbed, no."

The camera lit on her. Full face, live, her eyes sparkled.

"Do you mean to tell the American people, live on "Friday Night," that you have never, not even once, coached a witness to do anything illegal?"

"No, I never, not even once, did anything illegal in my life, except crossing the border of Hungary."

"Why," she continued, "do you, Mike Folsom, mean to tell the American people that "Friday Night Live" knows otherwise?"

Folsom beamed, victorious.

"Well, I have someone here who I'd like you to meet."

And with a Vegas swivel to the right, he announced: "Ngobi! Ngobi Shururu! Please come in."

The Ethiopian woman whose rights Kay had once defended, materialized and sat next to Kay.

Shururu confirmed that, a few years back, when she invited her sister to the States, Kay Kemeny had advised her not to tell Immigration that she was coming here to live. She had advised her to say she was entering only as a witness to a trial. She even wrote a letter to invite the sister to that trial, and on that basis the sister got the visitor's visa. Shururu followed Kemeny's advice and everything turned out all right.

When she was finished, Folsom turned to Kay.

"You're seeking one of the most important posts in this country. One which requires honesty and ethics. You have sworn to that as a lawyer. You have sworn to abide by the law. How do you explain then coaching a witness to mislead, in fact to defraud the Immigration and Naturalization Service of the United States? Isn't that illegal, Ms. Kemeny? Doesn't that make you a criminal?"

Lights, cameras, action, all focused on her.

Kay ignored them. Instead, she turned to Shururu and spoke to her in a soothing, warm voice, forcing the camera to close in on both of them.

"How have you been, Ngobi?"

It was so anti-climactic that Folsom was too stunned to intervene. By the time he did, it was too late. The bond between the two women was sealed.

"Ngobi, I've got a problem and you can help solve it. I'm asked by the President of this wonderful country to never let anything like what happened to you and your sister in Ethiopia happen to anyone in the United States."

"And then," she turned to Folsom, looking at him as if he were miles and miles away, a mere insect without consequence, "people like this man here do everything in their power to stop me."

Ngobi's eyes filled with tears.

"I'm sorry."

Folsom cut in.

"You advised Shururu to lie to the U.S. government. Isn't that a crime? Couldn't you be disbarred for this crime? And you ask Congress to confirm you?"

"One thing you could do now to clear this up, Ngobi," Kay continued, ignoring Folsom. "Tell us who made you tell all these lies about me."

"They made me," Ngobi pointed vaguely to the dark corners of the room, as if she could see invisible ghosts. "I can't say more, they hurt us if I say."

"Who will hurt you, Ngobi? Who?" Kay asked in a steady, calming cadence.

"They hurt my sister if I say."

"Ngobi, don't be afraid." Kay took her hand in hers. "Tell me."

Tears sprung from the Ethiopian woman's eyes as she spoke.

"Immigration man with FBI man. Two men came. Show badge, say they know about my sister. Say my sister criminal and liar, say she have to go back to Ethiopia. Say he take my green card too, and throw me out of the America. I'm scared. Very scared. And then —"

"Then?" Kay asked soothingly. At that moment Folsom wished Kay was on his side.

"They say I say this about you. All this I say. And they let me alone. And they let my sister alone."

"I ask, what happen to Ms. Kemeny if I say. He say nothing happen. Just small thing, politic, nothing bad. I'm sorry."

"And so it is, Mr. Folsom." Kay said, sadly, rising to leave. "You must have paid top dollar."

Kay left the studio without another word. She put Ngobi in a taxi and gave her Senator Endicott's and her direct lines, just in case. This was mainly to reassure her. She knew that after tonight Ngobi and her sister would be just fine.

She was glad she did the show now. She had not wanted to risk a live confrontation this late in the game.

But then Tommy and Jacobi told her what was in store.

The news of the smear was shocking. Who wanted her out so badly? Jacobi wouldn't say. She suspected he knew more.

Tommy mapped out the FBI surveillance on Shururu so that Jacobi could slip through and prepare her. He did a good job convincing the woman that she had nothing to fear.

Ezra Jacobi.

This man she hardly knew had saved her career for the second time. His emergence in her life, the way he accepted to stay with them and help after Stevie was deeply moving. There was a sense of ready compassion and a rare warmth about him, despite his many reservations. This man with one foot in another world, a frightening world, guided her like a glowworm, sending light in the dark, showing her the way. She felt safe when he was around.

She trusted him.

* * *

The next morning, in a rare Saturday statement, the Department of Justice announced that there was no evidence any officers of the administration had played an official role in the Shururu/Kemeny affair.

* * *

Wade Jennings stood at the table in the center of the second floor at the warehouse he had rented for the Kemeny mission.

A single light hung above him, illuminating the detailed, three-dimensional plan of the street in front of the Regency Excelsior and a minutely detailed map of the area linking the hotel to the White House. It was all perfect, he was sure. Racklee had prepared it.

This was the ninth termination he handled for Racklee, but it was the first woman. Racklee had said it was critical to the national security.

He had thought it through, but he still couldn't shake a feeling of uncertainty. It was damned foolish to narrow the hit down to one night.

At least Racklee had planned for two attempts. One following the reception and one just in case she stayed late with the President.

Jennings looked up at the three young, muscular men standing before him. To the novice, they were three middle class blacks, neatly attired in their gray slacks, navy blazers and rep ties, perhaps professional athletes? To the trained eye they were three fine specimens of military poise. Three Amer ican commandos.

"$200,000 each," Jennings told the men, "half now and half after."

The former Navy Seals stood silent.

"The objective is to terminate the target and escape."

EIGHTEEN

"Nobody tells you about betrayal in advance."

The voice came clear, crisp, loud, from every direction.

"Nobody warns you what will happen after you finish playing your role."

Racklee had been summoned to this spot just an hour before — a deserted airport strip near the edge of the great swamp, a cemetery for airplanes, with no attendant in sight.

There was still a semblance of a runway in the ruined airfield, good enough to hold a small private plane.

"I know you don't trust me, Grigor," Racklee shouted, his voice losing its timbre, swept up and dissolved into millions of separate sounds by the wind. "But you're wrong."

"Can you hear me?" he cried louder.

The only sound that came back was his echo.

"It's not my fault. It's CIA. They fucked up again. Don't worry. She will not get confirmed. Grigor, do you hear me?"

Not a single sound, other than his own voice and the hush of morning wind getting stronger as the sun slowly made its astral appearance from beneath a thin film of cloud.

"Do you hear me?"

No answer.

Vorody was playing games. Vorody didn't trust him anymore. And that meant he could no longer trust Vorody.

He turned to go.

"Lieutenant, you and I have unfinished business."

The voice came from behind, making the back of his neck bristle. Racklee turned abruptly and froze.

The man before him was not Grigor Vorody.

"Who the hell are you?" he barked.

"Look out there, Lieutenant," the stranger pointed to the city. "What do you see?"

"What did you do with Vorody?"

"You know, I'd always rather look at a city than go in it. You no longer see things once you're inside. Same with our cause, you and me."

Damn this. It was Vorody's voice. And the words — Vorody's words. What the hell —

"Vorody. Is that you?"

"No, Edwin. Not the final me. Just a version for now. One I can afford to let you see."

Racklee could not believe his eyes. Platinum blond hair, white in places, like an albino's. Skin bleached. White eye lashes and brows, over yellow gold eyes, tinged with red. A different point to the nose. A different Vorody. Who would ever look for someone so conspicuous?

"Did you have surgery — so quickly?'

"No, Edwin," he laughed, showing a new set of teeth. "I haven't decided on a permanent face yet."

Racklee wondered for the hundreth time what he would give to trade places with Vorody. Even now, as he readied himself to be hunted for the rest of his days Vorody was so much bigger, so much more of a hero than he. Vorody spent his life on the firing line. And he could turn into anything he wanted to be. Vorody was free.

"We will terminate her before confirmation. You have my word."

"Forget it, Lieutenant. The damage is done. My face is everywhere."

"It will stop here. I will not let it go further. Change your face and your papers and you'll never have to worry about this again."

"And the President?"

"He doesn't believe we're involved. Even if he did, he wants to see the Republicans covered with this dirt."

"I may have what you need to make Stone stop her."

"Too late now, Grigor. Believe me. Whatever it is you have, it's too late. Nothing can make him withdraw her after last night."

"I have something that could. I owe it to Nicholas to try."

"Let go, soldier. The dead come to haunt you only if you ask them. Stop asking him in."

Through some kind of sorcery an object materialized in his hands. He gave it to Racklee.

"Take a good look at this, Lieutenant. It's my gift to you. The last insurance. This will give you magic powers. For as long as Stone is President, you will be more powerful than he."

"And you?"

"I'll fade away. I might be back to haunt you, Edwin. Will you invite me?"

Racklee clutched the video tape in his hands, wordless, until the plastic case gave in, making a crackling sound.

"I gave you glory on a platter, Lieutenant. And now I'm ready to take it away. As long as I'm alive you're safe. Pray, my friend. Pray for me."

He walked away into the distance until he reached a spot, far away, where Racklee could now distinguish the shape of a small military plane.

The mass grew bigger and passed him just in time to see through it a flash, one last flash of the man who spoke and sounded like Grigor Vorody.

* * *

Martha's Vineyard

At least they left him alone this afternoon.

Millicent was off with Leduc on a lifestyle interview. George was at the ball game. And Krone left him playing tennis before lunch with the new communications assistant. Twenty seven tops. Sweet. Very blonde. He got her off the court as soon as possible and they toured the estate he had on loan from his friends. He felt old.

He missed Kay.

And now he had to sit in this dark study which reminded him of his office, waiting for a certain Jennings from CIA's Clandestine Operations.

He had received a call early this morning from the Director of Operations, requesting they meet without delay.

Jennings showed up a little after 4 pm. He had a video tape.

"What is this about?"

"Mr. President," Jennings answered in a grave voice that made him uneasy. "It's best to see."

Roger slipped the tape in the video player, but Jennings insisted he leave before it started.

On the screen there was the 1972 promo clip which ran on the networks in various formats, as a documentary, and later as a presidential campaign commercial. The American Hero Against PLO Story.

Stone looked at Jennings.

"I already saw that footage, Jennings. I hate to disappoint you."

Jennings motioned him to look on.

The tape went blank for a few seconds and then black and white, shaky footage started. It looked home made, showing a man's back which at first blocked the camera, and the awkward angle of a woman's face. Tall, dark hair, very long and thick, and the face — first the eyes, then the corner of her mouth, then the strong nose —

"My God."

Stone's pulse accelerated and his head started to spin. He was watching himself and Leila Khaled.

"Who taped that?" he asked in a voice even he couldn't recognize.

Jennings did not say a word.

The tape played further showing him standing above Leila. She was low on her knees and from the swing of his body and the way his head jerked to the right and left you could tell she was performing oral sex.

There was no sound. The recording was mute.

The frame was cut sharply to a full front shot.

My God he was young. His hair was darker, harsher, thicker. His waist was narrow and his skin white as snow. He was talking, animated, smoking, taking swigs from a bottle of Tuborg beer. Now and then Leila entered the picture and hugged him, covering half of his face.

Cut again.

Leila's hand entered the picture and gave him a newspaper. It was a copy of the *Herald Tribune*. She pointed at something and he started to read it out loud. The top of the newspaper entered the frame. The date was inked in very fine print but watching it Bob Stone knew, and so did the CIA experts who must have zoomed in already, that it was May 9, 1972.

"Stop. Stop it," he said. He started to rise.

"There's more," said Jennings.

The young man in the clip tucked his hand into his vest pocket. It was a beat up brown leather vest. From it he pulled a small packet of ID cards with indistinguishable photos and the large letters PRESS stamped across. He laughed and held them back, until Leila's hands entered the frame, one fondling his crotch and the other taking the press passes. Her face followed, covering again half of his, but then, surprisingly, turning towards the camera for a tight two-shot. Was he dreaming or did she wink?

He stared at the blank screen and pulled open his shirt. Two buttons fell noisily on the armrest.

He held his naked chest with one hand, trying to control his heart. He was cold all of a sudden. Very cold. He closed his eyes.

"You didn't know she was PLO," said Jennings.

The answer came almost inaudibly.

"I thought she was a journalist from Israel."

"They used those press passes to bring in the weapons."

Jennings walked slowly to the video player and removed the tape. He placed it back in his briefcase.

Bob Stone opened his eyes and straightened himself in his seat. He pulled his shirt together and buttoned it.

"This is terrible," he whispered.

"Yes."

"Jennings."

"Mr. President."

"Who else has this tape?"

"We can only guess."

"Do, please. Guess."

"It came in our possession as a bargaining chip in the case of a man who is a former KGB. He does not wish to be pursued."

"Go on."

"This man lives in the United States. He bargained years ago for our protection. If he is found, the former KGB will destroy him."

"Do they have the tape?"

"If they had, they would have sold it back to us years ago. No. No one else but Grigor Vorody."

"Grigor Vorody?" Stone seemed shocked.

"He wants you to stop Kay Kemeny."

* * *

"All right Bob. Let's think. And let's stop being silly. You have a certain relationship with her. A certain...affinity. If you explained, if you told her everything, wouldn't she want to back off to save your presidency?"

"She's stubborn, Mill. She's obsessed with that bastard."

"What if you withdrew her without her consent?"

"She'd go nuts with the press. She'd start the scandal of the century. This is bigger than what it seems."

"You're saying she's out of control."

"She is." He looked away. "I'm sorry."

Millicent rose and turned to the fire. The artificial flames released no heat. No comfort.

"Don't think I don't know what this will do to us Millie. And to your plans to run for —."

"That's nonsense Bob. That should be our last worry. Right now I'm just the First Lady. And from the looks of it, that's all I'll ever be."

She turned back to him.

"Can't they stop Vorody?"

"Jennings says he's too clever."

"No way to make him bargain for something else? Other than this nomination?"

"No. He just wants me to get rid of her."

Her eyes narrowed and her body tensed. She paused for a long time before asking:

"What does Jennings propose?"

"He... he asked permission to handle it."

Millicent's eyes traveled to the wide-open window. The night outside was pitch black and gusts of wind played havoc with the fire. The curtains blew in.

She looked at her husband again with a kind of pity.

Her voice was distant and remote when she spoke:

"Well, then. Maybe you should let him."

NINETEEN

Kay arrived just before midnight.

She was taller than usual on black stiletto heels and an unexpected black evening gown.

"I'm rehearsing!" she laughed seeing the puzzled look on his face.

"For what?" He caught her by the narrow strap of her dress and pulled her to him.

"For the party!" His lips grazed hers and she closed her eyes, dizzy with the sensation.

"Are we going anywhere?" he asked and looked down at his bare feet.

"Tomorrow we are."

He seemed surprised.

"Tomorrow is the reception, remember? The White House reception for the Italian Foreign Minister? The start of my confirmation hearings? Could it be you've forgotten the most important day of my life?"

But his hands were already on her breasts. The four days they spent apart had made his desire infinite, unquenchable.

"I'm worried about Vorody, Kay," he said later, when her head was resting on his shoulder. "I've...I've heard rumors. Frightening rumors, about KGB wanting to stop you and Vorody being close by."

"Who from?" she asked, indifferent. "Someone, no doubt, wants to frighten me."

She waved his words away like smoke. But he had broken the spell. She sat up and curled away from him.

"I'm not my father's daughter for nothing, you know. We don't back down from fear in my family."

"Why risk your life when communism is dead?"

She didn't know whether to smile or cry. Was he that naive? Did he really believe her fight was over?

"Don't worry, Stone. The KGB has no reason to come after me."

"How about Vorody?"

"He can't. He has the police everywhere in the world looking for him. He'd have to be crazy to roam about Washington just for revenge."

"That's not what my sources tell me."

He looked at her for a long time, and she held his eyes.

"Would you marry me, Kay," he asked, suddenly. "If I were free?"

She had to grab for balance when she rose and sat up, her back to him. She could still feel the imprint of his fingers on her skin.

"No."

"Why not?"

She swung back toward him and looked him straight in the eyes.

"Because I want to love you desperately."

She broke into a smile. But he went on, looking tense, strange, unbecoming.

"I thought one day I could divorce. And I fear for you. I can't really talk about it, but trust me. My advisors tell me that this nomination is very dangerous for you." He caressed her hand.

"Why not withdraw, my love? Start again later. When it's safe. I'll make sure you get the opportunity. I could never forgive myself if something happened to you."

"What does this have to do with marriage, Stone?"

"I don't want to lose you."

"You can't be serious."

She started to dress quickly, angrily.

"Why are you so upset?"

He seemed surprised.

"Because you assume, you always assume that you can have me. Anytime you are ready. And that you can put my life on hold until then.

"You and I can never marry, Stone, because you refuse to understand that I do not depend on you. That I depend on no one. That I can get up now and walk away. Sure I'll be miserable for a while, but so what Stone? I can walk and I will walk every time. You think love is something you can hold against me? I will not wait around until you're free to abandon your wife and child. And I will not wait around until the country doesn't give a shit about what you do anymore.

"I would not give up this opportunity if I knew KGB was waiting for me at the street corner. You think I would let them or you or anyone else intimidate me?"

She looked at him as if she was seeing him for the first time. "I love you Stone, but I don't think I could respect you if you walked out of your commitments for my sake."

He didn't reply.

She turned away to wipe a torrent of tears. She felt lost. Was it possible that this was it then? Was it possible that she will never again be touched, held, loved by this man?

When she looked at him again, his face was blank, remote, the passion that had been there before a memory.

She kissed him good-bye and he wiped, gently, a tear from the corner of her eye.

"See you tomorrow," he whispered, and she nodded.

"Yes. Tomorrow."

* * *

Kay walked back to her hotel with Roger close behind.

The air outside had cooled considerably, as if a wisp of chill passed through the early September, reminding everyone that the countdown was over. Summer had come to its inevitable end. She shivered in her strapless dress and clutched her shoulders. It was a good thing this was a short walk.

She turned the corner toward the hotel, immersed in the riddle of Stone's behavior. Why did he suddenly ask her to withdraw? And why did he suddenly propose?

She stopped just as the well lit front of the Regency Excelsior appeared in plain view. Something unusual was going on.

She glanced to her right. Roger was still there.

She looked more closely. Three young black thugs stood at the sidewalk curb, between her and the doorman. She looked at Roger again, but he didn't seem worried. She relaxed.

She went up to her room and thought to call Ed Endicott. But it was late and she was exhausted. She fell into a dark, oblivious sleep.

* * *

Wade Jennings watched the rehearsal through a thick pair of army binoculars — Racklee's gift for an old successful termination.

He checked every inch of the zone they had picked to hit Kemeny and nodded. Nothing out of the ordinary.

Tomorrow the stolen car will be around the corner, just out of sight, when the target arrives.

He'll wait, his cellular phone in hand, across from the White House and signal when Kemeny starts on her walk home. The car will pull up slowly. Inside will be his two best Seal shooters.

The Seal "drug dealer" will walk up to the car and jive with the shooters as they monitor the target's walk towards the two homeboys. They knew nothing about the hit. They were paid to protect him.

The dealer will stand in front of the rear window, blocking their view.

As Kemeny comes behind, the driver will give the signal and the dealer Seal will move to the hood side of the open window, leaving an open path between the men in the car and the two homeboys. The driver will shoot them with a Mac 10, making sure they are neutralized before he and the man at the back go on to shoot Catherine Kemeny. It will be nothing more than the usual "spraying" of the scene during a drug shootout.

Yes, Jennings thought, five seconds, just about. By the time she hits the pavement the dealer will be in the front seat. And the car will drive off to the pizza delivery van four blocks away. The police will find in it shell casings, dope and other evidence that will confirm this was a drug deal gone bad.

They will question the only surviving witnesses at the scene, an elderly German couple, tourists, frozen in shock, who will tell about the group gathering there every night for the past few days, just around the time they took their evening stroll, and about how the shoot out unfolded.

The dry run went smoothly.

The operation was on for tomorrow night.

* * *

From atop the roof of a four-story building across the street from the Regency Excelsior, the incandescent red cross of a telescopic lens pointed exactly at Kay Kemeny's forehead, as she entered the hotel.

The man holding the scope to his eyes was in his late thirties, brown hair and a droopy lip, which put a permanent sneer on his face.

Of course, a drug cover was better than a downright hit. But Kemeny dead was the *mot d'ordre* here.

Bartlett said the woman could not be allowed to survive.

TWENTY

"Kimberly's back in Washington."

Stone turned to his wife.

"What?"

Just then a familiar charge shot through his body.

"Ah, our guest of honor," he said, hoping his voice sounded steady. "It's so good to see you, Ms. Kemeny."

Kay smiled, giving him her hand.

"Thank you, Mr. President."

Millicent watched.

Stone's eyes followed Kay around the room.

She was moving toward the Attorney General, Ed Endicott at her side. He watched as the Italian Foreign Minister, Arturo Ceriani, a tall, extremely handsome man of fifty, approached her. Even from a distance, he could see his dark, worldly eyes linger on her body. He felt a stir of jealousy. She wore her favorite color, ivory. A simple, strapless sheath of lace, feminine and sensual. She glanced his way. Those sunny eyes always seemed just a touch wet, a touch vulnerable. She wore almost no makeup and her tanned skin glowed bare, as if sprinkled with an invisible gold dust. Her lips were moist, her hair flew freely in big, thick waves, the color of chestnuts and honey.

He looked past her to Millie and caught her eye. They were remote and still, but she blinked twice and in that flutter he guessed a kind of sympathy.

He shivered.

Suddenly Millicent looked behind him, startled, just as the White House master of ceremonies announced:

"Mrs. Larry Devane."

Kimberly Devane looked heavier than usual, puffy and disheveled in a gold lame gown which pulled heavily at the thighs.

"Ladies and gentlemen, may I have your attention please."

To everyone's applause, the President stepped on the low dais.

"We welcome a very special guest tonight, the Honorable Arturo Ceriani." He smiled engagingly as the Italian Foreign Minister joined him.

"He has been here less than two days and yet he managed to understand all about America — by being part of our favorite weekend, Labor Day."

Ceriani congratulated Stone for the creation of the Human Rights post.

Stone bowed to renewed applause.

"It's great you mentioned that, Mr. Ceriani," he said. "Because we are also celebrating tonight Kay Kemeny's confirmation hearings. They're starting tomorrow. And she is here with us. Kay, will you come up here please?"

He finally touched her again. He was sure her pulse was as fast as his when he held her hand.

Kay gave a brief speech. He felt foolishly happy when she said, "I must praise from the bottom of my heart our President." Everyone applauded. Kay shone among them like a precious jewel and she was his. She was still his.

"Well, isn't that nice."

Every head in the room turned.

"You get a job, he gets a blow job."

The crowd parted, making room for Mrs. Larry Devane.

"Speak to me Bob, don't stand there like a dickless bull, tell me, wasn't it better when you laid sweet ol' Kimmie?"

Kimberly advanced, unsteadily, through the speechless crowd. When she stopped, Stone could hear the hum of the air conditioner and the ice clinking in Millicent's punch glass.

Kimberly wobbled onto the small stage and grabbed the microphone from Kay, whose warm smile remained painted on her lips.

"That's right, folks. I loved him, I gave him what his wife can't, and then this foreign bitch comes and takes him away.

"I hope you're sorry now about what you've done to me, Bob Stone." She reached deep into her purse, her body trembling visibly. She pulled out a small pistol.

"I hope you're sorry."

In a fraction of a second, a secret service man tore the weapon from her hands and another grabbed her, and threw her over his shoulder. Her legs kicked the air and her purse fell, red pills dropping like pebbles on the marble floor. By the time the door closed behind her, the rustle of her dress and the echo of her last words were the only sounds alive in the room.

Millicent caught the desperate eye of Clancy Leduc.

She looked at her husband, ignoring the tears that streamed down her face. He put down his glass and started toward her.

From behind, a hand touched her shoulder.

"Signora Stone, this is a pity for such a nice evening, but you know, women when they drink...passion, bad words. All this is such a common thing in Italy, even in our politics."

Ceriani took her hand to his lips and kissed it.

"You will see, Signora, all this is not true."

He looked reproachfully at Stone.

"You'll be all right, Signora Stone. All of us men are... hmm, well, only human. But in America, you have to learn a little to relax. What do you say? Please, cara Signora, please." He wiped her tears with his handkerchief.

Leduc interrupted.

"Mrs. Devane has been under great stress. The President, you see, is a very warm man. Mrs. Devane clearly misinterpreted his affection."

"Of course," interjected Ceriani, "so warm, charming, and so brilliant!"

"All right. Clancy, Arturo, you're both so kind. So very kind." Millicent touched their hands and smiled. "Thank you. And now let me apologize to our guests."

Millicent pushed the two men gently to the side and went to the dais.

"I must tell you all how sorry I am. Especially for my husband. This is all so unfair to him. Kimberly Devane is very sick. She's a victim of substance abuse and depression. Sadly, this is something we've been very aware of for some time. She just returned today from the sanitarium, obviously too soon."

Everyone in the room gathered around her. Stone stood alone, forgotten. Across the room, he saw Kay approach the Attorney General, and he watched the Attorney General turn his back on her. Yes, my love. You have me to thank for this. She turned to him and her eyes asked the question. He met them for a moment, then shook his head. No, my love. I can't.

He watched her move toward the exit and saw the press storm after her. "What will you do now, Ms. Kemeny?" they called out at her. "Any comments Ms. Kemeny?" And he watched her turn to them, her face a mask of determination.

"I am withdrawing my candidacy for the human rights post."

He went to the window. It was misty, fogged, as if suddenly winter had taken summer away.

He saw Kay walking alone towards the street, her head thrown back, looking up at the sky. Free.

"I love you Kay," he whispered, his breath making a huge circle on the glass.

He turned to watch his wife on her platform, composed again, shaking hands like a good hostess, embracing each guest as they slowly began to leave.

Tomorrow, he will apologize to Millicent.

He will turn The Library into a study for George.

He will allocate $50 million to drug and alcohol addiction programs around the country.

And there will be no more videotape.

No more Vorody.

* * *

At 8:45 that night Ezra Jacobi and Tommy O'Hara were having beers at a nearby bar in Washington

"One more night and she's in," said Tommy. "So now that's done, pal, I still want Stevie's killer. Are you going to tell me who did it?"

"It's easy, 'pal.' I can't tell you what I don't know." This was one lie that made him feel good. If he told Tommy who it was he'd sure as hell get killed long before he could nail Bartlett in Wiesbaden. "Besides, O'Hara, even if you do, you can't bring them to court. They own Justice."

"Why? Did you indict the terrorists who killed your people?"

"We were at war."

They sat silent.

"Did you ever kill a man, Tommy?"

"Once. A shoot-out in a bank robbery."

"They were firing at you?'

"Yes. There were hostages. It happened fast."

"When you find Stevie's killer, he won't be standing with a gun to someone's head. There will be no lives to protect, no hostages. And he won't be shooting at you. He'll be eating breakfast or sleeping, or walking into his house with a bag of groceries. You'll be just a few feet away, close enough not to miss. You will have two seconds to aim and shoot. You'll try to make it two bullets at the back of the head so you never have to see that face in your dreams. But you know what? He'll probably turn and stare at you just the same. Then you'll have to pull that trigger and put a bullet right between his eyes. And you'll know that it was you, Tommy, just you alone."

He paused and took a long sip of beer. He wiped his mouth with the napkin, folded it, and looked back at Tommy.

"Could you do that?"

The answer came rushing at him.

"Damn straight, I...I.." but he didn't finish. He looked away.

"And another thing. Your target is an American agent. This guy did a thing or two for your country, just like you and me. He killed Stevie because Stevie threatened the national security. He did his job, even if it was ugly."

Tommy lowered his eyes.

"Whoever killed him has to pay, Jacobi. I don't care if they did it for Motherland."

Jacobi's beeper went off. He looked at it and saw on the small screen Antoine's number. He looked back at Tommy. What more could he do? He had warned him. The kid had to chill out. How did the English say it?

Revenge is a dish best eaten cold.

* * *

145

The phone rang in the red Chevy parked four blocks from the Regency Excelsior. The driver nodded when Jennings said:

"My date is on her way, alone."

He passed the message on, by phone, to the dealer and his two homeboys.

* * *

Antoine answered on the first ring.

"I got something that you should know, Ezra. I'm not sure how it's tied to what you're doing, but it's Washington. And it's Bartlett."

"I'm listening."

"Last week Papa caught one of our guys in Hamburg doing some business on the side. He needed a few days off. Turns out he and his wife got a contract from a Bartlett in Wiesbaden, to go to Washington for a job. The job is tonight."

"What job?"

"Witnesses."

"When? Where?"

"D.C. That's all they knew. Oh, and another thing. They're staying at the Regency Excelsior. Not far from the White House."

Jacobi hung up and raced back to the table. It all made sense. Bartlett sends witnesses from Wiesbaden. To the Regency Excelsior. And tonight is the night before confirmation. That's it, dammit.

"Get up Tommy. We're leaving."

"Where to?"

"Kay's hotel."

* * *

The Navy Seal from the rear seat opened the trunk of the red Chevy, took out a large duffel bag and climbed back in. He removed from the bag a smaller pouch and handed it to the driver.

The driver opened it and pulled out the MAC 10, re-checked it, cocked it, took off the safety, and slipped it back under the bag on the front passenger seat facing the window, within easy reach.

The Seal in the rear did the same with his AK-47 and settled with it in his lap across the center of the back seat.

The weapons were well hidden. The target would be in plain view.

* * *

The Frenchman saw the three drug dealers arrive and take up their positions on the street. It was early. Could it be that something had gone wrong?

146

He stepped back to his case which lay open on the matte black tarpaulin spread out to capture the shell casings.

On the tarp was his bolt-action, sharpshooter's rifle, loaded with three hollow point bullets. The telescopic sight was accurate, he checked it two hours before. He checked it again.

By now, he could shoot the target with his eyes closed, in the dark. Aim at the head, shoot twice. Swivel 180 degrees. Kneel and place rifle on tarp in front of the case. Separate clip, silencer, scope, barrel and stock. Place each piece in its custom cut depression in the case. Roll up tarp and stuff in case. Close and lock.

Ninety seconds max.

Leave, re-locking the door to the rooftop behind. Down the stairs, out the rear exit. Take off the gloves. Start to walk.

Two minutes in all.

He took his 9-mm semi-automatic pistol from his shoulder holster and placed it on the cornice. A heavy weapon, made cumbersome by the long silencer. A necessary evil — his rifle could not shoot with precision anything at a close distance. He needed a hand gun.

If all goes well, no one gets near him and the gun goes back unused.

* * *

"The Europeans do it this way, you see?" Jacobi explained to Tommy in the car.

"You know there's a hit when they ask for witnesses. It only works for street hits, or anything in public places. They plant credible witnesses who then give false leads to the police. It's how I know they won't kill her in her room at the hotel. No, it will be the street. Definitely the street. We'll cruise the street that starts at the White House, all the way to the hotel. We'll look for an elderly couple. When we find them, we'll follow their eyes."

"I see," Tommy said in disbelief, with one hand on the wheel driving at 80 miles an hour, and the other on his redial button trying to call the FBI.

"But how do you know this whole set up is for her?"

"My boy," Ezra replied, "you smell it, that's it. You don't have time to cover your ass. By the time the FBI asks for an explanation we're dead. But go on. Make your call."

Just then the connection went through.
"FBI unit C55, Supervisor Murray."

Tommy glanced at Jacobi.
He hung up without a word and dialed three digits.
"911 police emergency"

He picked up and cupped the phone with his hand, disguising his voice.

"This is an emergency of the first degree. Foreign agents are planning to assassinate a high government official near the Regency Excelsior hotel in the next few minutes. One federal agent is there and needs help. Perps presumed KGB."

TWENTY-ONE

Kay walked through the windy night.

She had known she was not his first lover. She had heard the rumors about Kimberly. Stone's women. She had joined their ranks.

And Millicent — she was extraordinary. Half victim, half conqueress. Condemned to half happiness.

She couldn't remember Stone. She couldn't capture him in her mind's eye.

Worse things happen you know, Mother would say, and she'd be right. Think of your father.

Tony would gloat. I was right wasn't I? You made a spectacle of yourself.

You can't win them all, no, you can't, I know that, Uncle Daddy. You lost so much more than me.

She listened to her steps. The wind had changed direction, and hit her straight in the face. She turned to look behind at the glorious lights framing the White House.

"I'm not setting foot in that place again."

Her voice vanished in the wind.

The clouds gathered in thick layers, blanketing the sky. The moon disappeared. It was colder, much colder than a minute earlier. She wrapped the long shawl tighter around her chest and shivered.

How could she have missed it?

Was she blinded by her belief that everything was clean and good in America? Not wanting to see that her dreamland, the promised land, was just as decayed as the rest of the world?

Why was Vorody so important to the Americans? Why so important as to want to protect him, to stage the smear, to threaten even the President, to make him ask her to withdraw, to make him fear for her life. What did they have to hide? Who was he?

She was truly alone and apart in some strange place. Like a Polaroid fading fast before her eyes, America disappeared, leaving behind the contour of a dream.

* * *

The dealer was entertaining his homeboys with drug stories. He noticed the same elderly couple leaving the hotel, and heard fragments of their conversation. German. Then he spotted the red Chevy, coming toward the street corner.

"Stay loose," he told the two men. They patted their 9-mm pistols confidently.

He went to the car, leaned against the front passenger door and poked his head in.

"I can see the target."

She walked alone, her hair undone, lean and graceful, wrapped in a sheath of fabric which lifted at her back with each step she took, like wings.

With a sigh, the Navy Seal in the back raised his AK-47 just below the car window. Two hundred thousand dollars was good money these days. Business was getting scarce in his line of work. Why get sentimental?

The driver propped his MAC 10 in position. He didn't like thinking of the victim before a shoot.

The dealer reached inside his loose jacket to unlock the safety of his .45 pistol. The target was a white bitch, like the rest of them.

* * *

The driver whispered, "15 seconds."

His eyes followed the target through the windshield.

She was still in front of them. She had to come to their passenger side to give them the right angle. And she had to walk by the two homeboys to get into the line of fire.

"Ten seconds."

A black Ford pulled loudly to a stop right in the curb, between the Navy Seals and their target.

Jacobi, on the passenger side was the closest to the Chevy. But O'Hara, younger and more agile, was out of the car faster, spinning around to the front, onto the sidewalk, his ID already up there in his left hand and his .38 service revolver in his right. He stood between the killers and Kay, drawing a bead on the leader.

"Federal Agents," he yelled, "clear the street, assholes, NOW."

He pocketed his ID, cocked his pistol, took a two-hand grip and moved forward toward the Chevy, swinging his gun from the homeboys to the Seals.

"I said move this shit box out of here NOW, motherfuckers! Don't fuck with me!"

Kay stood frozen.

Jacobi came out of the car low, crouched below the Chevy's hood, moving quickly to his right until he was about 15 feet away in the street. He lifted his .32 mm Beretta. The men in the car had their backs turned and their weapons pointed the wrong way, towards the shooting zone. Jacobi had them within a two-inch sweep of his gun. He couldn't miss.

The dealer looked past the occupants of the car and saw Jacobi targeting his teammates.

He did nothing.

None of the three men moved.

Good, thought Jacobi. Professionals. There won't be any blood tonight. They're keeping their cool. They must have more firepower than us but they're smart enough to know we got the shooting angles. Okay guys. Time to abort. Don't disappoint me.

Out of instinct, he kept scanning the scene. Nothing out of the ordinary. He glanced briefly at the old couple across the street — but he wasn't worried about them. Hired witnesses never interfered with a hit.

He looked up. The moon, hidden the entire time, suddenly appeared behind a cloud, illuminating something new in the darkness. Something he hadn't seen before.

There was no movement inside the red Chevy.

"She's still too far back," the driver said quietly to the dealer. He spoke without moving his lips.

"No good sight lines on any of them," reported the man in the back seat.

The leader took in the scene. He saw the two homeboys dashing around the far corner, taking with them the drive-by shooting pretext.

He made his call.

"Abort."

His physiognomy changed immediately, and he turned to face O'Hara, his hands high, open and empty.

He started to jive.

"Hey, man, yo, sheet man, I gots the right to rap with my homeboys, ya know, man..."

He went on like this a few seconds longer, with Tommy pointing the gun directly at his face, daring him to make the wrong move.

"All right, man, you're the Man, you got the piece, we're goin' man, sheet..." He climbed into the front seat. The red Chevy backed up, spun a U-turn and shot away, leaving behind a thick trail of smoke.

Tommy didn't move until the car left his sight.

He lowered his weapon and sighed. Thank God. They had rescued her. He turned. Kay's face was the color of her dress, transparent, bloodless.

But wait a minute — Tommy stopped. Something was wrong. Something was missing. His eyes swept the street. Where was Jacobi?

He spun around, instinct telling him that the night had some other horrible turn to play. He screamed at the top of his lungs, "Kay! Get down! Kay!" He sprinted to her. She was so close, just 10 yards away, yet he was running in slow motion, 9 yards, 8, 7, it felt like his body weighed a ton. Shit, man, this was like running through water. What was happening to him? He pumped his legs like pistons, 5 yards, 4, still slogging. He couldn't warn her anymore, he couldn't take the time to speak. Tommy coiled his right leg and lunged forward, high into the air, his chest rose for a split second over Kay, his hands reached for her head, taking her down with him onto the ground. The last thing he heard before he fell unconscious was the jarring sound of the first bullet splitting the air.

Jacobi's legs hurt like hell, his heart punched at his rib cage and sweat poured into his eyes, blinding him, by the time he reached the rooftop. He banged the tin door open just in time to hear a shot. Some bastard up here was shooting at Kay and Tommy.

He wiped his eyes with the back of his hand. Now he could see him. To the left, a backlit silhouette, against the cornice.

He ran, but running was hard on the gravel, it was slippery and every step he took made a loud, screechy noise. Come on you fuck, he encouraged himself, moving fast toward the assassin's back. Just three more seconds and you're mine. He rushed forward aiming at the same time, when the killer suddenly turned.

The long rifle fired just as he lost his balance, skated on the gravel, and fell forward on his belly.

The bullet shaved his head.

"Merde," he heard the killer say.

Merde my ass, Jacobi whispered. He's got me.

But no shot came. The Frenchman dropped his rifle, grabbed his pistol and cocked it. Jacobi didn't wait. He pushed his belly down and flipped, rolled on his back and fired twice, upside down, straight into the man's torso. He lay on his back, his fingers clutching the trigger. He took his time to see that the Frenchman was down, and that his pistol had fallen out of reach. He checked himself to see if everything was in place, no blood anywhere around him. He was fine. He sighed, relieved. He was all right.

He got up.

The Frenchman on the other hand didn't look so good. He lay on his back, clutching his stomach with his hands, a steady trickle of blood streaming from his mouth. He hadn't made a sound. Not a scream, not a sigh, nothing. Tough to the end.

"You should have aborted, pal," Jacobi said, kicking away the silencer gun, even though it didn't look like the Frenchman could use it now. No answer came. Blood flooded the pavement around him.

The poor fuck.

He pointed the pistol at his head. But his hand stopped on the trigger. It was too late for mercy. Someone could hear the shot. Jacobi turned to look down at the street.

He could hardly see Kay. She was covered by Tommy, except for her head and feet. She lay face up, under the marquee lights, her eyes closed, like she was asleep. Blood leaked from her head and from Tommy's chest in every direction, soaking the asphalt, shiny, un-natural, like spilled paint. He wiped his forehead with his left hand and felt his fingers shake.

And he, Ezra Jacobi, as always, stayed alive. Middle-aged, seen it all, freelance navigator through Spookland for whoever paid the price.

He put down his gun and watched the ambulances pull at the curb, spilling out an army of men dressed in white.

I'm not sure I want this, God, Jacobi said to the black sky, holding both hands together to stop from trembling. I'm not sure I want this anymore. You're like a cat, Jacobi, Stevie once said. You always land on your feet. That's right, pal. I'm just a fat cat born under a lucky star.

Four police cars lined up in front of the hotel and a flock of uniforms emerged near the bloody patch where Kay and Tommy lay in their final embrace.

The mask of death had already spread over their paid assassin when Jacobi turned to look at him again.

"You should have aborted, you shit," he said, not sure if he could still hear him.

The Frenchman moved his head a notch. Up, then down. Did that mean get lost, asshole, I'd shoot you right now if you put a gun in my hand? Or could it be that he nodded, yes, I should have aborted, I made a mistake and now here I am.

Look at this fuck, Jacobi thought, wiping a tear he had felt coming ever since he looked at Kay and Tommy on that pavement. He killed his friend and he killed the brave lady he was trying to help. Lots of help he had been to them, really. He would have been better off never giving them those damned photos. Better off not saving her from that smear. Better off if they never met.

Look at this fuck. Now that he was giving his last breath even he looked human. He wasn't sure why, but he knelt down beside the killer and raised his head in his arms. He felt his body tense in a final spasm.

"It's never easy to kill a man, Tommy. Not even this one," Jacobi whispered. Look at him now, look at his features. Death was slowly wiping the snarl off his face. It was becoming serene, properly lined, nose to mouth to eyes all the way to the hairline. Human. The Frenchman was being set straight, at last.

* * *

He came down the stairs and into the street.

There were cops everywhere, roping the area, taking prints, talking to the witnesses.

He tried to go around them to get to the ambulance. But he was stopped.

"I was with them," he told the officer, showing him his private investigator ID. "The killer was professional. A Frenchman, I think. He's dead, up there on the roof."

The cop gestured to his men to check it out and took Jacobi's Beretta out of his waist band.

"Look, give me a moment to check the ambulance. They were my friends. I'll be back. I promise."

The haggard man gave him a weary look.

"Let him go, sarge, he was with them. He's the good guy!" cried the hotel doorman.

The cop nodded.

"OK. Go."

Tommy must have been wheeled in the ambulance that just left because now they were bringing Kay up into an empty one, paramedics hovering over her, an IV drip hooked to her arm.

He ran to the ambulance and caught her eye just as they were lifting her on the ramp.

"Wait!" he shouted. "Wait a minute!"

He climbed up with her.

Her eyes were vague but she was conscious.

"Baruch Ha Shem, thank you God," he prayed, "please, please, let her stay alive long enough for them to take that bullet out."

He didn't realize he had talked out loud until one of the medics answered:

"There's no bullet there, Sir, she just cracked her head on the sidewalk. It's the guy that got shot."

"Is he still alive?" Jacobi asked, crushed by a grief that had been clutching his heart ever since he looked down from that roof.

"He's critical, but alive. They tore him up pretty bad."

Jacobi wiped another tear just as it was starting, and looked at Kay. He took her hand in his.

"He'll make it, Kay." A smile, more real than anything he thought he could muster, traveled on his face. "That Irish boy will make it every time."

She moved her hand to her mouth weakly and, with a superhuman effort, soaking the white bandage on her head in a new wave of blood, tore the oxygen mask off.

He could hardly hear her when she whispered:

"Who did it, Ezra? Who did this?"

Jacobi couldn't speak. What good will it do you, pretty shiksa, if you knew? The bets are off, the game has played out, the corpses line the pavement. You almost became one. But you're alive. Despite me.

154

He bent his head down and looked straight into the dark, blood-stained floor that mapped so many endings. All right God, I was wrong and you were right. Don't let your good intentions mess with people's lives, you told me. You feel better and they die. What kind of good is that, Jacobi? I guess the road to hell is paved with spooks, God. And I'm one of them.

He looked at Kay. Her eyes were fading fast.

"Who was it, Jacobi?"

There is no altar for this sort of thing, he thought, touching her forehead lightly with his fingers. But if I have to sacrifice a lamb right now to keep this woman alive, I will. I'll sacrifice the truth.

"The KGB, Kay," Jacobi said. "Who else could it be?"

Mikaela Mar and Daniel Aharoni

About the Author

DANIEL AHARONI is a Manhattan attorney, counsel to a private intelligence agency, and author of a satirical newsletter published within the intelligence community.

MIKAELA MAR is a Manhattan fashion publicist, free-lance writer and former magazine editor.

www.ingramcontent.com/pod-product-compliance
Lightning Source LLC
Chambersburg PA
CBHW020516290526
45786CB00002B/617